the CRUCIFIED LIFE

SEVEN WORDS FROM THE CROSS

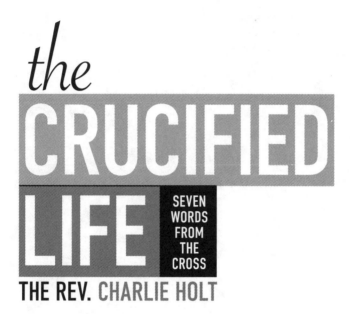

THE REV. CHARLIE HOLT

EDITED BY GINNY MOONEY

Bible Study Media

The Crucified Life: Seven Words from the Cross

© 2014 by Charles L. Holt

Published in Lake Mary, Florida, by Bible Study Media, Inc.

Printed in the United States of America

Interior design by Lonnie G. Creative

Hardcover Black and White ISBN: 978-1-942243-03-8

Paperback Black and White ISBN:978-1-942243-01-4

Hardback Full Color ISBN: 978-1-942243-17-5

THE CRUCIFIED LIFE

CONTENTS

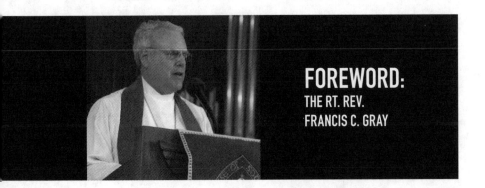

FOREWORD:
THE RT. REV. FRANCIS C. GRAY

The Reverend Charlie Holt has greatly expanded the traditional *"seven last words from the cross"* into an extraordinary and deep Lenten Group Bible study program. With depth of research and breadth of material, Fr. Holt has compiled a body of work which will be helpful and timely for years to come. Rather than exploring the words from the cross only on Good Friday, the author uses these timeless passages as a framework for all of Lent. Fr. Holt includes supplemental material from hymns, works of art, and other helpful illustrations. All of this is held together with well-thought-out exposition from the author's considerable Biblical knowledge. When Good Friday arrives, the reader is prepared for this most solemn day of the Church Year.

Father Holt's writings display the work of a person of faith who is also a theologian and Biblical scholar. He is a frequent contributor to the ongoing concerns and issues of the current church. His writings are important to the debates about Church and culture. His writing is refreshingly clear and direct. His teaching not only follows the received tradition of the Church but also reflects the Old Testament understanding of prophetic discourse. He calls the Church back to the covenantal roots of the faith, rather than encouraging trendy and innovative theology.

This study, well suited for individual and for small group use is refreshing, solid, enlightening and deeply Christ centered. One only hopes that there will be future offerings from this gifted priest and author.

+Francis C. Gray
Retired Bishop
of Northern Indiana

INVITATION: THE CALL TO A HOLY LENT

Dear People of God:

The first Christians observed with great devotion the days of our Lord's passion and resurrection, and it became the custom of the Church to prepare for them by a season of penitence and fasting. This season of Lent provided a time in which converts to the faith were prepared for Holy Baptism.

It was also a time when those who, because of notorious sins, had been separated from the body of the faithful, were reconciled by penitence and forgiveness and restored to the fellowship of the Church. Thereby, the whole congregation was put in mind of the message of pardon and absolution set forth in the Gospel of our Savior, and of the need which all Christians continually have to renew their repentance and faith.

I invite you, therefore, in the name of the Church, to the observance of a holy Lent by self-examination and repentance; by prayer, fasting, and self-denial; and by reading and meditating on God's holy Word. And, to make a right beginning of repentance, and as a mark of our mortal nature, let us now kneel before the Lord, our maker and redeemer.

The Book of Common Prayer (BCP), p. 264-65

This Lent, you are invited to take a journey into the heart of the crucified life. Jesus challenged His disciples more than once to *"pick up your cross and follow Me."*

And [Jesus] said to all, "If anyone would come after me, let him deny himself and take up his cross daily and follow me."   **Luke 9:23**

Notice the word "daily," which is included in the verse from Luke's Gospel. Taking up our cross daily does not mean literally dying every day, of course. It is appointed for us to physically die on one appointed day. However, Jesus calls his followers to a daily discipline and focus on self-denial illustrated by the image of "taking up the cross."

The period of Lent is a 40-day journey of self-denial. Through *"self-examination and repentance; by prayer, fasting, and self-denial; and by reading and meditating on God's holy Word"* (*Book of Common Prayer*, p. 265), we are invited by the Church and the Lord to individually and corporately prepare ourselves for the annual celebration of the death and resurrection of Jesus during Holy Week and Easter. We accomplish this through a concentrated time period of "taking up our cross."

The 40-day period begins with the service of Ash Wednesday. Here we acknowledge our finite and mortal nature. "Remember that you are dust, and to dust you shall return." While speaking these words, the priest applies ashes to our foreheads in the Sign of the Cross. As disciples, we are marked for crucifixion—taking up our own cross.

The message delivered during an Ash Wednesday service is often related to the last words Jesus uttered from the cross. The four Gospel witnesses—Matthew, Mark, Luke, and John—testify that Jesus spoke seven distinct times from the cross:

- *"Father, forgive them, for they know not what they do."*
  Luke 23:34

- *"Truly, I say to you, today you will be with me in Paradise."*
  Luke 23:43

- *"Woman, behold, your son!...Behold, your mother!"*
  John 19:26–27

- *"I thirst."*   **John 19:28**

- *"My God, my God, why have you forsaken me?"*
           Matthew 27:46

- *"Father, into your hands I commit my spirit!"*   **Luke 23:46**

- *"It is finished."*   **John 19:30**

Traditionally, these seven sayings have been associated with seven words:

FORGIVENESS • SALVATION • RELATIONSHIP • DISTRESS ABANDONMENT • REUNION • TRIUMPH

Each week during Lent, we will reflect on one of Jesus' seven final utterances from the cross. Each day I will offer a focused reflection on one aspect of that week's saying. The seven last sayings of Jesus are jewels of great value, and worthy of our gaze, deep meditation, and reflection.

My prayer for you during this Lent is that you and I will walk daily toward the cross with humility and purpose. I look forward to seeing how God will use this offering of ourselves to Him. Please let me or any of the other clergy know how we may serve you in this season of your spiritual growth in Christ Jesus our Lord.

As I am faithfully yours in Him,
Charlie Holt+

INTRODUCTION: CHRIST DIED FOR ME

In my experience as a pastor, I have discovered that many well-meaning Christians have trouble with the idea that Jesus is the only way to the Father. As Jesus Himself taught, "*I am the way, the truth and the life; no one comes to the Father except through me.*"

The difficulty comes when we begin to think of people whom we love dearly—friends and family—who have not yet believed in Jesus, or, even more difficult, those who have died without giving any indication of belief or saving faith in Him.

Have this mind among yourselves, which is yours in Christ Jesus, who, though he was in the form of God, did not count equality with God a thing to be grasped, but emptied himself, by taking the form of a servant, being born in the likeness of men. And being found in human form, he humbled himself by becoming obedient to the point of death, even death on a cross.

Therefore God has highly exalted him and bestowed on him the name that is above every name, so that at the name of Jesus every knee should bow, in heaven and on earth and under the earth, and every tongue confess that Jesus Christ is Lord, to the glory of God the Father.   **Philippians 2:5-11**

Paul makes it abundantly clear why Jesus is the only way and why there is no other name through which salvation might be found in Heaven or on earth. Why? Because Jesus is the one God chose to use to forgive the sins of humanity through His own self-sacrifice.

Salvation is only in Jesus Christ, for it is because of His death on the cross that God has exalted Him to the highest of places, to be the King of Kings and the Lord of Lords. He humbled Himself and became obedient unto death. Therefore, it is only through Him and in His name that salvation may be found.

Jesus died for the sins of the world. He did it willingly, and He did it personally for you and for me. The Apostle Paul says, *"Jesus Christ died for me."* Paul put himself at the foot of the cross. Likewise, this is what you and I are called to do, place ourselves at the foot of the cross and say, "Jesus Christ died for me."

When the great preacher Charles Spurgeon was nearing his death, he shared with a close friend, "My theology now is found in four little words: 'Jesus died for me.'" He went on to say, "I don't say this is all I would preach if I were to be raised up again, but it is more than enough for me to die upon."

The hymn *"And Can It Be"* by Charles Wesley, another great preacher, captures the depth of emotion believers experience when applying the cross to ourselves. Take a moment to meditate on the words:

And can it be that I should gain
An interest in the Savior's blood?
Died He for me, who caused His pain—
For me, who Him to death pursued?
Amazing love! How can it be,
That Thou, my God, should die for me?
Amazing love! How can it be,
That Thou, my God, should die for me?

He left His Father's throne above
So free, so infinite His grace—
Emptied Himself of all but love,
And bled for Adam's helpless race:
'Tis mercy all, immense and free,
For O my God, it found out me!

'Tis mercy all, immense and free,
For O my God, it found out me!

Long my imprisoned spirit lay,
Fast bound in sin and nature's night;
Thine eye diffused a quickening ray—
I woke, the dungeon flamed with light;
My chains fell off, my heart was free,
I rose, went forth, and followed Thee.
My chains fell off, my heart was free,
I rose, went forth, and followed Thee.

Still the small inward voice I hear,
That whispers all my sins forgiven;
Still the atoning blood is near,
That quenched the wrath of hostile Heaven.
I feel the life His wounds impart;
I feel the Savior in my heart.
I feel the life His wounds impart;
I feel the Savior in my heart.

No condemnation now I dread;
Jesus, and all in Him, is mine;
Alive in Him, my living Head,
And clothed in righteousness divine,
Bold I approach th'eternal throne, and
Claim the crown, through Christ my own.
Bold I approach th'eternal throne, and
Claim the crown, through Christ my own.

If Christ died for us while we were sinners, consider the attitude we ought to have toward one another. Paul said our mindset should be exactly the same as that of Christ Jesus. The heart of Jesus Christ is a posture of grace and love; the heart of the follower of Jesus Christ ought to be the same.

We pray in the Lord's Prayer every single Sunday: *Forgive us our trespasses, as we forgive those who trespass against us.*

That prayer is a very dangerous prayer. You cannot pray that prayer unless you have first placed yourself at the foot of the cross and allowed Jesus to pray to the Father, *"Father, forgive them, for they know not what they do."* Say the words, *"Forgive our trespasses, as we forgive those who trespass against us,"* and any unforgiving judgment against another in our hearts becomes a petition for God to judge us. Yikes!

Underscoring the dangerous line from His Prayer, Jesus reveals that He really did mean for us to take that line seriously as He goes on to teach:

For if you forgive others their trespasses, your heavenly Father will also forgive you, but if you do not forgive others their trespasses, neither will your Father forgive your trespasses. **Matthew 6:14-15**

Our greatest barrier to intimacy with God is our lack of forgiveness toward others. As you think about what Jesus has done for you on the cross, consider this: "How in the world could I personally hold a grudge or withhold forgiveness from any other person on this planet?"

Place yourself at the foot of the cross and allow Jesus to work His grace into the deepest parts of your soul—His forgiveness of us leads to our forgiveness of others.

Then the petition from the Lord's Prayer comes from the heart, and we can say to God:

Father, I forgive, as you have forgiven me.

WEEK ONE
THE FIRST WORD
FORGIVENESS

"Father, forgive them, for they know not what they do."

Two others, who were criminals, were led away to be put to death with him. And when they came to the place that is called The Skull, there they crucified him, and the criminals, one on his right and one on his left.

And Jesus said, "Father, forgive them, for they know not what they do." And they cast lots to divide his garments.

And the people stood by, watching, but the rulers scoffed at him, saying, "He saved others; let him save himself, if he is the Christ of God, his Chosen One!"

The soldiers also mocked him, coming up and offering him sour wine and saying, "If you are the King of the Jews, save yourself!"

There was also an inscription over him, "This is the King of the Jews." **Luke 23:32-38**

DAY 1
ASH WEDNESDAY
FATHER, FORGIVE THEM

Mental health counselors often encourage their clients to learn how to forgive themselves. It is true that we are often our own worst critics and judges. However, the problem with this well-meaning counsel is that we are manifestly not the ones to offer forgiveness to ourselves.

Even if we were able to somehow attain a more charitable attitude toward ourselves, which is not a bad thing, this attitude would be completely inadequate to truly heal and restore us. The real need that every one of us has is to understand and receive the gift of God's forgiveness. In the Psalms, David writes to God, *"Against you, and you only have I sinned."* He is expressing the truth that all sin and wrongdoing—even that which is directed toward other human beings—is ultimately against God Himself. That is why God must be the one to forgive us. True freedom from sin and guilt can be found only in Him.

Ash Wednesday calls us to remember our need for God, as well as our finite and sinful nature. We are tangibly marked on the forehead with the sign of the cross in dirty black ash. God formed man out of the dust of the ground (Genesis 2:7). As creatures, we are limited and finite—*"Remember that you are dust."* The mark is also a reminder of the fall of humanity into sin. We have rebelled against the loving command of God and forfeited a vital relationship with

God. As a consequence, we are now given to an inevitable, ignoble death as mortals: *"...and to dust you shall return."*

Ash Wednesday does not leave us in the dust, however. It is also the day we begin the season of Lent at the throne of grace. The Lord invites us to the table where He gives us another firm reminder—one of grace, redemption, and restoration. In the bread and wine, we mysteriously commune with the body and blood of our crucified Savior. Through the Sacrament, we remember what He has done for us in bearing in His body the finite and mortal nature of man. By becoming one of us and like us in our death, God has made it possible for us to become like Him.

Before going to the cross, Jesus *"took bread and when he had given thanks, he broke it and gave it to them, saying, 'This is my body, which is given for you. Do this in remembrance of me.' And likewise the cup after they had eaten, saying, 'This cup that is poured out for you is the new covenant in my blood'"* (Luke 22:19-20).

Let that good Word connect with you personally—Jesus is speaking to you. He said, *"...poured out for you."* The blood of the New Covenant is for the forgiveness of your sins. Believe the words of Jesus and stop doubting His love for you.

When you receive the body and blood of Jesus Christ, you begin approaching the foot of the cross and the throne of grace. Today, open your ears and your heart to hear the prayer of Jesus spoken on your behalf:

Father, forgive them, for they know not what they do.

The reality of God's forgiveness of your sins is as real as the black ashes marked on your forehead. Jesus' death on the cross is an historic reality that takes away from you the mortality and sin that the black ash represents. Jesus' love and forgiveness of your sin is as real as the sacramental bread and wine you consume.

Rather than trying to forgive yourself, taste the Lord's words of forgiveness for you. Inwardly digest His love for you. Believe and receive the gift of forgiveness and love.

REFLECT:

Why is forgiving ourselves not enough—why do we need God's forgiveness? Jesus said his blood was poured out for you, to forgive your sins because He loved you. If you grasped this truth more fully, how would it change your life? Ask for His help today.

_____

_____

_____

_____

_____

_____

_____

_____

_____

DAY 2
THURSDAY
THE BLINDING EFFECT OF SIN

In his letter to the Romans, the Apostle Paul describes the human condition: "*For although they knew God, they did not honor him as God or give thanks to him, but they became futile in their thinking, and their foolish hearts were darkened*" (Romans 1:21).

Theologians refer to the noetic (intellectual or mental) effects of sin. What that means is that human sin and rebellion against God have corrupted our minds and destroyed the lively sensitivities of our hearts. Jesus intercedes: "*...they know not what they do.*" Sin had so corrupted their minds and their hearts that the people who crucified Jesus did not even fathom the gravity of their own actions. They could not see their own evils; they were blind to their own sin. That is how corrupting sin can be. It can corrupt us to such a degree that we cannot see, believe, or realize that we are, in fact, sinning.

This is true in each of our lives. One of the key reasons I need other people in my life—other caring Christians—is that they can actually see my sin very clearly. I am often blind to my sinful actions. I simply don't see them, but others can see these sinful actions and help me recognize them and bring them to the cross for forgiveness and repentance.

In the Sermon on the Mount, Jesus asks, *"Why do you see the speck that is in your brother's eye, but do not notice the log that is in your own eye?"* (Matthew 7:3).

Jesus knows us all too well. He knows we tend to minimize our own sin and maximize other people's sin. The Lord would call us to turn our vision back toward ourselves. *"Or how can you say to your brother, 'Let me take the speck out of your eye,' when there is the log in your own eye? You hypocrite, first take the log out of your own eye, and then you will see clearly to take the speck out of your brother's eye"* (Matthew 7:4-5).

Jesus prayed: *Father, forgive them, for they know not what they do.*

What did the people of Jerusalem do? Instead of praising Jesus, they mocked Him. The soldiers offered Him sour wine and said, *"If you are the King of the Jews, save yourself."* A cynical inscription was even placed over Him: *"This is the King of the Jews."* By clothing Jesus in the royal garments of a king, His crucifiers actually had it right. He was the King, though they did not acknowledge it. After they crucified Him, they cast lots to divide these very garments.

Father, forgive them, for they know not what they do. What did they do? Three words: They crucified Him. The most evil action ever committed by humanity was done that day—in sinful ignorance, they crucified the Lord of glory.

How can this corrupt mental understanding, that continues today, be remedied? The Apostle Paul says:

> *But we impart a secret and hidden wisdom of God, which God decreed before the ages for our glory. None of the rulers of this age understood this, for if they had, they would not have crucified the Lord of glory. But, as it is written,*
> *"What no eye has seen, nor ear heard,*
> *nor the heart of man imagined,*
> *what God has prepared for those who love him"*

AND WHEN THEY
CAME TO THE PLACE
THAT IS CALLED THE
SKULL, THERE THEY
CRUCIFIED HIM...
LUKE 23:33

—these things God has revealed to us through the Spirit. For the Spirit searches everything, even the depths of God. For who knows a person's thoughts except the spirit of that person, which is in him? So also no one comprehends the thoughts of God except the Spirit of God.

1 Corinthians 2:7-11

The blindness and corruption of our minds and hearts can only be reversed by the power of the Holy Spirit. Great humility is required to admit our mental and spiritual need.

REFLECT:

Have you ever asked God to fill you with His Holy Spirit? The path to knowing God and ourselves is through the inward filling of the Holy Spirit of God. In your prayer today, ask God to search your mind and heart through His Holy Spirit for any sin or darkness, and, by the same Holy Spirit, ask for comprehension of the thoughts of God.

_____

_____

_____

_____

_____

_____

_____

_____

_____

DAY 3
FRIDAY
THE INACTION OF JESUS

And the people stood by, watching, but the rulers scoffed at him, saying, "He saved others; let him save himself, if he is the Christ of God, his Chosen One!"

The soldiers also mocked him, coming up and offering him sour wine and saying, "If you are the King of the Jews, save yourself!"

Luke 23:35-37

In the context of this first saying from the cross, the narrative tells us that the rulers and soldiers taunted Jesus, encouraging Him to do something, to vindicate himself, to act. *"He saved others; let him save himself,"* and *"If you're the King of the Jews, save yourself."* Even one of the criminals hanging next to Jesus derided him saying, *"If you're the Christ, save yourself."* Three times people challenged Jesus to do something—to save Himself. Over and over again, in various ways, they were saying we want to see you do something.

Here is the irony of those taunts: what would have happened if Jesus actually did what they challenged Him to do? If, following the ignorance of humanity, Jesus actually had chosen to save Himself?

First, there would be no forgiveness of sins. By his inaction, by refusing to save Himself, Jesus opened the door of salvation to all sinners. Consider the words of the prophet Isaiah:

Surely he has borne our grief
and carried our sorrows;
yet we esteemed him stricken,
smitten by God, and afflicted.
But he was pierced for our transgressions;
he was crushed for our iniquities;
upon him was the chastisement that brought us peace,
and with his wounds we are healed.
All we like sheep have gone astray;
we have turned—every one—to his own way;
and the Lord has laid on him
the iniquity of us all.   **Isaiah 53:4-6**

By doing nothing and remaining silent to their calls for action (like a sheep before its shearers), He was able to accomplish our forgiveness.

Also, if Jesus had done what they urged and saved Himself, that very action would have resulted in the Day of Judgment for all of humanity. For Jesus to call down the armies of Heaven on His own behalf would have surely meant a most fearsome and awesome judgment from God. Why? Because they were sinning against the Son of God.

They didn't know what they were asking! They didn't recognize it, but they were committing the most grievous sin that a human being has ever committed—rebelling against the supreme authority, the God of Heaven. Humanity was killing God in the flesh. Concerning this, the Apostle Paul wrote:

For in him all the fullness of God was pleased to dwell, and through him to reconcile to himself all things, whether on earth or in heaven, making peace by the blood of his cross.
And you, who once were alienated and hostile in mind, doing evil deeds, he has now reconciled in his body of flesh by his death, in order to present you holy and blameless and above reproach before

him, if indeed you continue in the faith, stable and steadfast, not shifting from the hope of the gospel that you heard, which has been proclaimed in all creation under heaven, and of which I, Paul, became a minister.   **Colossians 1:19-23**

They did not know it, due to their "hostile minds" and "evil deeds," but they needed Jesus to disregard their words. They needed Jesus to not respond. So did we. His lack of action not only accomplished our forgiveness, but it also delayed the Day of Judgment so that many could repent.

In our frustration toward God, we at times accuse Him of inaction. The cross testifies that, in the very moment when God did not intervene with vindication of the Holy and Supreme Good, that is when His greatest redemption and mercy were accomplished.

God is forgiving, forbearing, and patient with us in our ignorance. *"The Lord is not slow to fulfill his promise as some count slowness, but is patient toward you, not wishing that any should perish, but that all should reach repentance"* (2 Peter 3:9).

God has given you and those you love the gift of time. There is a part of us that, along with the rulers, soldiers, and criminals of Golgotha, would love to see God act in a powerful way to vindicate His name. His inaction baffles us at times. Yet this is His love, and this is His grace—to wait on our repentance.

There will be a day coming when Jesus will display His mighty arm in great power, where He will come with the armies of Heaven. This Day of the Lord is in our future, but until that day, we wait upon the Lord.

REFLECT:

Are there areas in your life where you are frustrated by the inaction of God? Looking back on your life, have you ever seen where God's nonintervention has given space for redemption and grace for yourself or another person?

_____

_____

_____

_____

_____

_____

_____

_____

_____

_____

_____

_____

DAY 4
SATURDAY
THE ACTION OF JESUS

Yesterday, we looked at the inaction of Jesus on the cross, what He did not do. The dying Jesus did not call on God's power to save Himself. Today, we reflect on what Jesus did do on the cross.

He prayed for his persecutors.

Father, forgive them, for they know not what they do.

Instead of vindicating Himself, Jesus stayed the hand of the Father. Could it be that the Father was poised and ready to send the armies of Heaven to vindicate His Son and the only thing that stopped them from coming in awesome wrath and terror was the prayer of the Son?

Don't judge them. Forgive them. Give them grace. Show them mercy.

The very jeers, the very scoffs of the soldiers toward Jesus on the cross ironically revealed exactly who it was they were crucifying: The Lord of love and forgiveness.

I have found in my pastoral work that, if I really want to know what is on a person's heart, I should listen to their prayer requests. Have you ever been in a small group of Christians and talked for an hour, but when you ask for prayer requests, the real heart concerns and vulnerabilities are revealed? In the same way, Jesus reveals His heart for us through His prayer request.

How do you know the heart of God for you? How do you know that God loves and forgives you? What did the Son of God pray? *Father, forgive them, for they know not what they do.*

Paul writes in Romans chapter five:

...but God shows his love for us in that while we were still sinners, Christ died for us. Since, therefore, we have now been justified by his blood, much more shall we be saved by him from the wrath of God.
Romans 5:8-9

By the very act of Jesus' praying that intercessory prayer for us, asking for our forgiveness, God the Father demonstrated His abundant love for us by graciously granting his Son's request, withholding judgment—"*while we were still sinners, Christ died for us.*"

Think about this: Jesus died for you before you ever trusted and believed in Him. He loved you before you knew Him. He loved you while you were walking away from Him. He loved you while you rebelled against Him. He loved you while you were His enemy! God the Father loves you. Jesus' prayer and the Father's response prove it!

By the way, Jesus' prayer for us did not stop on the cross. By virtue of His resurrection and His office as High Priest, Jesus continues to make intercession on our behalf. The writer of Hebrews says:

...he holds his priesthood permanently, because he continues forever. Consequently, he is able to save to the uttermost those who draw near to God through him, since he always lives to make intercession for them.
Hebrews 7:24-25

Today, I want to ask if you have done that in your life. Have you put yourself at the foot of that cross and allowed that intercessory prayer of Jesus Christ—*"Father, forgive them,"*—to be a prayer that He prays on your behalf? He was praying it for you.

He still prays it for you whenever you sin, whenever you fail. He intercedes where you have sinned intentionally. He prays to help you overcome the blinding effects where your sin has prevented you from seeing the way forward through repentance. In His kindness, His grace, He is praying. While we were enemies of God, Paul says, Christ died for us. His grace has preceded our repentance.

Father, forgive them, for they know not what they do.

REFLECT:

What did Jesus pray for His persecutors while He was on the cross? How does that prayer relate to us? Read Jesus' prayer of intercession on your behalf as if it were spoken directly for you. It was. Ask Him to help you forgive those who have wronged you.

WEEK TWO
THE SECOND WORD
SALVATION

"TODAY YOU WILL BE WITH ME IN PARADISE."

One of the criminals who were hanged railed at him, saying, "Are you not the Christ? Save yourself and us!" But the other rebuked him, saying, "Do you not fear God, since you are under the same sentence of condemnation? And we indeed justly, for we are receiving the due reward of our deeds; but this man has done nothing wrong."

And he said, "Jesus, remember me when you come into your kingdom." And he said to him, "Truly, I say to you, today you will be with me in Paradise. **Luke 23:39-43**

DAY 5
SUNDAY
PARADISE LOST

Sometimes it's easy to forget. This world was originally created to be a garden paradise. Over the years, through our destruction of the natural order, through the devastation caused by wars, through selfish and shortsighted stewardship, we have gradually, and at times rapidly, eroded the beautiful earth that God created and intended for our pleasure and abundant life. The story is familiar.

And the LORD God planted a garden in Eden, in the east, and there he put the man whom he had formed. And out of the ground the LORD God made to spring up every tree that is pleasant to the sight and good for food. The tree of life was in the midst of the garden, and the tree of the knowledge of good and evil. **Genesis 2:8-9**

Those were the days of blissful innocence when the Lord God walked alongside Adam and Eve in the garden in the cool of the day. Genesis makes several points about this life before the Fall of man.

All was deemed good. Humans were called very good, as they were made in the image of God. There were plenty of resources, no scarcity or hunger. There was no deprivation, sickness, or death— only abundance and life! God dwelt openly in the midst of His people. He walked and talked with the first people. There was no separation or fear in the relationship between God and his creation, only love and provision.

And God provided for companionship and intimacy for human beings:

> *Then the man said,*
> *"This at last is bone of my bones*
> *and flesh of my flesh;*
> *she shall be called Woman,*
> *because she was taken out of Man."*
> *Therefore a man shall leave his father and his mother and hold fast to his wife, and they shall become one flesh. And the man and his wife were both naked and were not ashamed.*   **Genesis 2:23-25**

But then came the Fall, the disobedience of the first humans. When Adam and Eve deliberately sinned, not only did they lose access to the Garden of Eden, but they also lost many of the blessings that came from dwelling in that garden. The freedom of abundance was replaced with a fear of scarcity. Life gave way to struggle, pain, death, deprivation, hunger, thirst, toil, thorns, and thistles. Generosity of spirit and goodness gave way to covetousness, mistrust, theft, demand, jealousy, and war.

However, the worst loss of all was the loss of intimacy with God. Adam and Eve lost their innocence and were ashamed to be in the presence of God:

> *And they heard the sound of the LORD God walking in the garden in the cool of the day, and the man and his wife hid themselves from the presence of the LORD God among the trees of the garden.*
> *But the LORD God called to the man and said to him, "Where are you?" And he said, "I heard the sound of you in the garden, and I was afraid, because I was naked, and I hid myself."* **Genesis 3:8-10**

"*I hid myself.*" With the fall of humanity into sin, self-hiding became normative for all people. No longer could people walk with God in the cool of the day. God suddenly became fearful to humanity because of the reality of human shame.

"Shame is an emotion in which the self is understood to be defective, unacceptable, or fundamentally damaged. Shame is often confused with guilt, which is a related emotion, but distinctly different." [1] Whereas guilt says, "I behaved badly," shame goes a step further and says, "I am bad." With guilt, a specific behavior is viewed as unacceptable or wrong; with shame, the entire self is condemned.

Some people experience a false sense of shame. Those who have experienced traumatic events or have been victims of physical or sexual abuse are prone to shame, particularly if they blame themselves in some way. Shame can be a problematic emotion because it is associated with a desire to hide, disappear, or even die.

Some people lack a sense of shame when they clearly ought to have it. One thief hanging next to Jesus on the cross rebuked the other thief for mocking Jesus:

"Do you not fear God, since you are under the same sentence of condemnation? And we indeed justly, for we are receiving the due reward of our deeds; but this man has done nothing wrong."

Luke 23:40-41

The mocking thief lacked the fear of God because he lacked the proper shame for his own corrupt life. The other thief felt that shame and, in turn, asked Jesus to take pity on him, *"Remember me when you come into your kingdom"* (Luke 23:42).

The shame the thief experienced was legitimate for a life lived apart from God and in rebellion against His laws. Yet, when the thief made his plea to Jesus, Jesus answered him saying, *"Truly, I say to you, today you will be with me in Paradise"* (Luke 23:43).

Jesus' words to the thief on the cross signaled to him and to us the end of the power of shame!

Do you ever experience feelings of shame? Are there times when you just want to run, hide, or escape? Hide from other people? Hide from God? You are not alone. This is a consequence of paradise lost. All human beings feel shame, whether they acknowledge it or not, and whether it is legitimate or not.

But Jesus took your shame upon Himself—both the shame you may experience because of your own sin and the shame you may unjustly feel for another's sin toward you—in order to restore you to an intimate relationship with God, one without fear! He restores you to a place where you no longer have to hide from God, a redeemed and restored paradise in which you are no longer

SHAME IS AN EMOTION IN WHICH THE SELF IS UNDERSTOOD TO BE DEFECTIVE, UNACCEPTABLE, OR FUNDAMENTALLY DAMAGED.

ashamed before the Lord. He bore your nakedness and shame that you might be fully clothed in His righteousness.

REFLECT:

What is the difference between guilt and shame? When have you experienced a sense of guilt or shame? Christ wants to take both from you! Are you willing to let Him do that? You can ask Him right now. Release that burden to Him and take a moment to experience how freedom from shame, now and forever, feels.

_____

_____

_____

_____

_____

_____

_____

_____

_____

DAY 6
MONDAY
THE APPOINTED DAY

I once had a conversation with my grandfather, a self-professed atheist, when he was on his deathbed. "Papa, are you afraid to die?"

"No," he replied.

I said, "Are you looking forward to it, then?"

"No."

"Why not?" I asked him.

"Because there's no future in it!"

My grandfather was always a jokester. Only on that day, I was saddened by his deathbed humor.

Every single one of us has a day in which we are appointed to die. It's one of our destinies, the most common destiny. Both Jesus and the two thieves knew that the day they were crucified was the appointed day of their death. They knew: Today I am going to die.

The Bible names only two people who did not have an appointed day of death: Enoch, who was transported into Heaven, and the prophet Elijah, who was miraculously taken up into God's presence. But those are the only two people in the history of the world who have not died.

The rest of us all have a day that we share in common, the day that we will die. Every single one of us will experience it. And yet, when Jesus speaks a word to the thief on the cross, it is not a somber acknowledgement of his day of death. Rather, He says:

Today you will be with me in Paradise.

This is why those who first followed Jesus had no fear of death, but were actually looking forward to it! As Paul sat in a Roman prison cell and reflected on his own approaching death, he wrote:

For to me to live is Christ, and to die is gain. If I am to live in the flesh, that means fruitful labor for me. Yet which I shall choose, I cannot tell. I am hard pressed between the two. My desire is to depart and be with Christ, for that is far better. **Philippians 1:21-23**

ONLY TWO PEOPLE IN THE HISTORY OF THE WORLD HAVE NOT DIED.

Why is it a gain to die? Because, as Jesus promised to that thief on his cross, the day you die is the day you will be in the Paradise of Heaven with the Lord. Jesus said to him, Today you will be with me in Paradise.

It is hard to contemplate the reality of our own mortality. Many deny the reality until faced with a crisis moment such as a dire medical diagnosis, a traumatic life-threatening event, or the death of a loved one. Do you know that today you can face that appointed day without fear?

The marvelous gift of knowing and believing in Jesus is that, even though we will certainty die on our appointed day, Jesus promises to transform the day of our death into a day of glorious entrance into the Paradise of God!

I am Resurrection and I am Life, says the Lord.
Whoever has faith in me shall have life,
even though he die.
And everyone who has life,
and has committed himself to me in faith,
shall not die for ever.

As for me, I know that my Redeemer lives
and that at the last he will stand upon the earth.
After my awaking, he will raise me up;
and in my body I shall see God.
I myself shall see, and my eyes behold him
who is my friend and not a stranger.
For none of us has life in himself,
and none becomes his own master when he dies.

For if we have life, we are alive in the Lord,
and if we die, we die in the Lord.
So, then, whether we live or die,
we are the Lord's possession.
Happy from now on
are those who die in the Lord!
So it is, says the Spirit,
for they rest from their labors.

The Book of Common Prayer (BCP), p. 491

REFLECT:

As you contemplate your own mortality, what thoughts and feelings are evoked in you? What fears? How would your life change if you began to look at your Appointed Day as a Day of Glorious entrance into the Paradise of God and His awaiting embrace? You can, starting now.

_____

_____

_____

_____

_____

_____

_____

_____

_____

DAY 7
TUESDAY
KNOWING THE WAY

So what makes going into the heavenly realms, Paradise?

Do you remember when Jesus' disciples were troubled after He informed them that His time was short and He was going to be with the Father?

"Let not your hearts be troubled. Believe in God; believe also in me. In my Father's house are many rooms. If it were not so, would I have told you that I go to prepare a place for you? And if I go and prepare a place for you, I will come again and will take you to myself, that where I am you may be also." **John 14:1-3**

There is a place in the Father's house, in the heavenly realms, prepared uniquely for each and every one of us by the Lord Jesus Christ. Jesus identifies this place as Paradise. Today, we most often use the word Heaven.

Jesus reveals this knowledge to His disciples in order that their hearts would not be troubled. He reassures His disciples that Heaven will be a glorious and joyful place, wonderfully prepared and adorned for every single child of God who puts his or her faith in Him. Heaven is wonderful because it is the house of our Heavenly Father!

But as Jesus also makes clear, knowing and believing in the joys of Heaven is not enough; one also must know the way to Heaven. Jesus reassures His followers, *"You know the way to where I am going."* Thomas, often called Doubting Thomas, asks the million-dollar question (doubters are great at asking the right questions) when he says to Jesus, *"Lord, we do not know where You are going. How can we know the way?"*

Jesus replies with those well-known words:

"I am the way, and the truth, and the life. No one comes to the Father except through me."   **John 14:6**

Jesus boldly declares that the way to where He is going is Him. The path to Paradise is not a code of ethics or a lifetime of good behavior; it is Jesus himself. The reason the thief on the cross was given access to the Paradise of God was not because he was a good person or had completed more righteous acts than sinful acts, but because he knew and believed in The Way, in Jesus.

Whether we are talking about Paul, the thief on the cross, Doubting Thomas, or you and me, Jesus offers us direct access to a paradise of God's presence through faith in Him. This promise is guaranteed to those who have personally placed their trust in Jesus Christ as their Lord and Savior. Such assurance of salvation provides tremendous peace to anyone confronted with his or her own mortality.

The deathbed conversation I had with my grandfather was disheartening. However, a few days later, my younger cousin sat down and spoke with my grandfather from her heart. She shared with him how she had come to know that one day she would be in Heaven with the Lord. She also told him how saddened she was by the thought that he would not be there and how she longed to see him again. Then she shared The Way and urged him to give his heart to Jesus.

That day my Grandfather prayed to receive Jesus into his heart and gave his life to the Lord! It was not long afterward that his appointed day came and, by God's grace, because of the promise made to the thief on the cross, I have assurance that my grandfather heard the words of Jesus spoken personally to him: *"Today you are with me in Paradise."*

The thief's public profession of belief in Jesus and his simple faith-filled prayer, *"Jesus, remember me, when you come into your kingdom,"* were enough to gain him free access into the Paradise of God. On his appointed day, that man knew The Way to Heaven, as did my grandfather.

REFLECT:

Take some time to carefully consider in your own heart, do you yet know The Way—do you know Jesus?

DAY 8
WEDNESDAY
IT IS NEVER TOO LATE

With some people in our lives, it can be difficult to have assurance of their salvation. When we truly care for someone, we tend to speculate with concern, are they a lost cause? Particularly when we see a long pattern of consistently self-destructive behavior or hard-heartedness toward the Lord in a person, we are often left wondering, is there any hope for this particular person, Lord?

Similarly, I've met people who think this way about themselves. They say, "I've made too many mistakes," or "I have lived a life apart from God for so long that He would never reconcile with me." One man once told me, "Heaven wouldn't want someone like me."

The story of Jesus' encounter with the thief on the cross reveals a very different perspective.

The thief was given a privilege that only a very few people have had—the privilege of watching his Savior die for his sins. In that very moment of watching Jesus die, the thief placed his faith and trust in the blood of Christ that was being shed on the cross, and he made a confession of faith: Jesus, remember me when you come into your kingdom. And Jesus commended his faith and said to him,

Today you will be with me in Paradise.

The thief had that one moment with Jesus—one moment at the end of his life when he personally encountered the Lord. And that one moment was enough for him to repent, believe, and put his faith in the One who died for him. A final moment of faith, and the thief was welcomed into the Kingdom of God purely by God's unmerited favor through the death of Jesus.

This story gives us the assurance that, up to the moment of a person's last dying breath, anyone can make a confession of belief in Jesus as their Lord and Savior and hear these words:

Today you will be with me in Paradise.

As a pastor, I have seen it happen with many people. And I'm sure it will happen with many more before my time of service on earth is complete. It is always a joy to witness.

Yes—there is kindness and hope for the many who have not yet called on the Name of the Lord. As long as they have breath to call out to Jesus, it is not too late. It is not too late for you. The abundant life in Jesus begins the day that you call upon His Name for salvation. For God has promised:

Everyone who calls on the name of the Lord will be saved.

Romans 10:13

You may think, "I've blown it," or "I'm too old to really change," or "God would never receive the likes of me." Don't believe those lies for a moment! They are from the Enemy of your soul, not from the Lover of your Soul. You are not a lost cause to Jesus.

The prophet Jeremiah writes, *"For I know the plans I have for you, declares the LORD, plans for welfare and not for evil, to give you a future and a hope"* (Jer. 29:11).

REFLECT:

Is there someone in your life you've "given up on?" How about yourself? Allow the testimony of the thief on the cross to encourage you to pray for those you love and to call out to Jesus for your own salvation. If you've already begun a relationship with Christ, ask Him for a deeper experience of His love. He always says "yes" to an open heart.

_____

_____

_____

_____

_____

_____

_____

_____

_____

_____

DAY 9
THURSDAY
THE GIFT OF GRACE

Yesterday, we talked about the thief on the cross and his last-minute confession of belief in Jesus. We saw that Jesus accepted the man's dying prayer and assured him that he would be welcomed that very day into the presence of God, into Heaven.

The thief on the cross had no time to get his life in order. He had no time to go through spiritual disciplines, to spend some time working on his personal prayer life, or to teach Sunday school. Who knows whether he had even read the Scriptures?

Yet, we often think that we need to do such things to secure our place in Heaven.

In reality, Heaven is not something that is owed to us because of the good works we have done; it is given by the unmerited favor and grace of God, by virtue of what Jesus has done on the cross. And yet, we have a tendency to want to see Heaven as some kind of reward for our good behavior.

Among long-time faithful Christians, I have sometimes seen resentment toward a long-time faithful sinner who makes a last minute deathbed confession. Similarly, I have been asked on more than one occasion about the fairness of this message of grace.

Addressing this issue, Jesus told a story about workers who went out into a field hoping to be hired for the day. One group came early in the morning and agreed with the landowner upon a daily wage. They set off to work.

Midway through the day, another group came along and were standing around idle. The landowner said to these men, "I have work for you to do," and agreed with them for a daily wage. They, too, went to work. Then, just an hour before quitting time, yet another group of workers came by, and the owner of the vineyard put them to work as well.

When it came time to square up with all those workers, do you know what they got paid? The exact same amount. As you might imagine, the workers who had been hired at the beginning of the day felt a little bit of resentment.

And on receiving it they grumbled at the master of the house, saying, "These last worked only one hour, and you have made them equal to us who have borne the burden of the day and the scorching heat."

But he replied to one of them, "Friend, I am doing you no wrong. Did you not agree with me for a denarius? Take what belongs to you and go. I choose to give to this last worker as I give to you. Am I not allowed to do what I choose with what belongs to me? Or do you begrudge my generosity?"   **Matthew 20:10-15**

God is by nature merciful and gracious. None of us who labors for Him receives what we truly deserve, which is eternal separation from God because of our sin. Rather, by His grace, we receive His presence with us in this life and Paradise in the life to come. That is why living for Him is never a burden or something to complain about.

In our immaturity, we, like children, often cling to notions of fairness. We act as if those who have lived their lives apart from God and come to know Him later in life have somehow unfairly gotten away with something. Of course, what we usually covet in those moments is life-destroying sin and selfish pleasures. (And if it really was all that good, why did they ever turn to Jesus?) As one man who came to faith out of a destructive lifestyle said, "One day of my life now, knowing Jesus, is better than all the previous days combined!"

Remember, out of God's abundance of grace and generosity, the Lord has been anything but fair with us. Indeed, we most decidedly do not want Him to be fair with us! We do not want God to base our reward of eternal salvation on the basis of our works—for that would mean that no one would be saved.

As Paul writes in his letter to the Romans:

What shall we say then? Is there injustice on God's part? By no means! For he says to Moses, "I will have mercy on whom I have mercy, and I will have compassion on whom I have compassion." So then it depends not on human will or exertion, but on God, who has mercy.

Romans 9:14-16

All of us need God's mercy, whether we are speaking of one who lives an entire life for God or of the thief on the cross who repents with his dying breath. God will have mercy on whom He has mercy and compassion on whom He has compassion. The petition of the thief was a humble one. All he asked for was Jesus' consideration. But what he received was amazing grace.

Amazing grace, how sweet the sound,
That saved a wretch like me.
I once was lost but now am found,
Was blind, but now, I see.
Twas grace that taught
my heart to fear.
And grace, my fears relieved.
How precious did that grace appear
the hour I first believed.

Through many dangers, toils and snares
we have already come.
'Twas grace that brought us safe thus far,
and grace will lead us home.

The Lord has promised good to me,
His word my hope secures.
He will my shield and portion be,
as long as life endures.

When we've been here ten thousand years,
bright shining as the sun,
We've no less days to sing God's praise,
than when we've first begun.

The author of that beloved hymn, John Newton, was the captain of the slave ship African. Much later in his life, he would write in a little pamphlet entitled "Thoughts on the Slave Trade," an apology for "a confession, which … comes too late … It will always be a subject of humiliating reflection to me, that I was once an active instrument in a business at which my heart now shudders."

John Newton experienced God's amazing grace and knew that, though he once was wretched in his sins, he was now forgiven and his life was forever changed. Grace would lead him home.

REFLECT:

Which words of the classic hymn "Amazing Grace" connect to your heart most deeply? Why? Do you ever have a tendency to want to "earn" your salvation or see others earn theirs? Where does this come from? Reflect for a moment that God is being merciful by not giving us what we deserve; instead, he gives us His Amazing Grace.

_____

_____

_____

_____

_____

_____

_____

_____

_____

DAY 10
FRIDAY
TWO KINDS OF PEOPLE

The two thieves who were crucified on either side of Jesus represent two sets of people in this world: believers and mockers.

One of the thieves was a mocker. He picked up the anthem of the rulers and soldiers and spewed, "*Are you not the Christ? Save yourself and us!*"

Even as he dies on a cross, this thief mocks the One who could save him from eternal hell—at the very moment that Jesus is in the act of dying for him.

There are billions of people in this world and all are appointed for death, perhaps not as imminently as that particular thief, but nevertheless, they are appointed for death. And yet many mock the name of Jesus Christ. They reject the Savior even while that same Savior lovingly desires to rescue them.

Recently, there was a college professor in the state of Florida who asked his students to take the name of Jesus, write it on a piece of paper, and stomp on it. Then, the rest of the assignment was for the students to answer the question, "Why did you have a hard time doing that?"

But there was one student in the class who refused to participate. "I can't do it," she said. One student. Why not more? Why only one person in the class who refused to stomp on the name of Jesus?

The scornful and mocking thief, like the professor, characterizes far too many people. But fewer in number are those represented by the confessing thief assured of Paradise, like the one student who said "No." Jesus predicted this imbalance when He said:

Enter by the narrow gate. For the gate is wide and the way is easy that leads to destruction, and those who enter by it are many. For the gate is narrow and the way is hard that leads to life, and those who find it are few.   **Matthew 7:13-14**

The pressure is on for those of us who would publicly claim and courageously stand for the name of Jesus Christ, especially in our contemporary culture. Every day that goes by, our society becomes increasingly hostile to the Gospel message and to anyone who would buck this trend of hostility by his or her allegiance to the Lord Jesus.

Consider the words of Charles Spurgeon, the beloved pastor and theologian, as he reflects on this dynamic between the two thieves and, in particular, on the thief who confessed. Spurgeon writes:

[The thief] was surrounded by scoffers. It's easy to swim with the current. It's hard to go against the stream. This man heard the priests in their pride ridicule the Lord, and the great multitude of the common people, with one consent, joining in the scorning. His comrade caught the spirit of the hour and mocked also and perhaps he even did the same for a while. But through the grace of God, he was changed and believed in the Lord Jesus in the teeth of all the scorn. His faith was not affected by his surroundings; but he, dying thief as he was, made sure his confidence. Like a jutting rock standing out in the midst of a torrent, he declared the innocence of Christ whom others blasphemed. His faith is worthy of our imitation in its fruits.

He had no member of his body that was free except his tongue and he used that member wisely to rebuke his brother malefactor and defend his Lord. His faith brought forth a brave testimony and a bold confession. I'm not going to praise the thief for his faith, but to extol the glory of that grace divine, which gave the thief such faith and then freely saved him by its means. I'm anxious to show how glorious is the Savior that saved to the uttermost, who at such a time could save such a man and give him so great a faith and so perfectly and speedily prepare him for eternal bliss. Behold the power of that divine spirit who could produce such faith on soil so unlikely and in a climate so unpropitious. [2]

Centre panel of a Crucifixion triptych, 1490s (oil on panel), Master of the Virgo Inter Virgines, (fl.1470/1500)/ © The Bowes Museum, Barnard Castle, County Durham, UK / Bridgeman Images

Which thief do we represent?

Oh, that we had more people in our day and age who had the strength of character to go against the crowd, to stand up to our mocking culture through their character and behavior. Oh, that more believers who profess Jesus at church would profess Jesus publically to a needy world headed in the wrong direction.

REFLECT:

How would you have responded to the assignment to stomp on the name of Jesus? Would you have bowed to the pressure of your peers and the professor, or would you be like the one student who refused? You are called to be a light and a witness for Jesus Christ, willing to undergo even persecution for His name. Pray that God would make you strong and give you opportunities to shine boldly and brightly for Him!

_____

_____

_____

_____

_____

_____

_____

_____

_____

DAY 11
SATURDAY
PARADISE RESTORED!

This week we have been studying the second of the seven last words Jesus spoke on the cross, when He said to the thief, *"Today you will be with me in Paradise."*

We have looked at many of the implications of these words, including the way God's grace extends to any and all who put their faith in Him, even to their last dying breath. Also, we've seen how our entrance into Paradise is a gift of God's mercy and not the result of our good works.

Think with me about what it means to be with Jesus in Paradise. First, I would offer to you that Paradise, commonly called Heaven, is not our ultimate destination. The promise of the Scriptures is that when we die, we will go immediately to be with Jesus in Heaven. But there is yet another day awaiting us, and that is the day when the New Heavens and the New Earth will be formed. The Apostle Peter taught:

But the day of the Lord will come like a thief, and then the heavens will pass away with a roar, and the heavenly bodies will be burned up and dissolved, and the earth and the works that are done on it will be exposed…the heavens will be set on fire and dissolved, and the heavenly bodies will melt as they burn! But according to his promise we are waiting for new heavens and a new earth, in which righteousness dwells.   **2 Peter 3:10-13**

Notice from this passage that even Heaven will be destroyed! Our final and eternal destination will be not in Heaven, but on the New Earth in which righteousness dwells.

The day of the Lord is approaching—a day when those who have died and are in Heaven and those believers still living on earth will be gathered together as a united People of God. Those of us who believe will be given resurrected bodies, and we will live in the presence of our King—Jesus—as he dwells in our midst. The ultimate promise of Scripture and the hope of the Christian is not to dwell in Heaven forever, but for the resurrected body and the resurrected life on the New Earth.

In the meantime, those who die prior to the Day of the Lord go immediately to Heaven to be with the Lord. To be in the present Heaven is what Jesus called a Paradise of God. He says to the thief on the cross:

Today you will be with me in Paradise.

The Apostle Paul also was given a vision of the present Heaven. He called it the third heaven, the first and second heavens being the atmosphere and outer space. Here Paul describes it in the third person as something that was too glorious for words and too wonderful for him to boast about:

I know a man in Christ who fourteen years ago was caught up to the third heaven—whether in the body or out of the body I do not know, God knows. And I know that this man was caught up into paradise— whether in the body or out of the body I do not know, God knows— and he heard things that cannot be told, which man may not utter.
2 Corinthians 12:2-4

The Apostle John was also taken up to the heavens in a vision. In Revelation 6, John records seeing martyred saints petitioning God from beneath the altar: *"O Sovereign Lord, holy and true, how long before you will judge and avenge our blood on those who dwell on*

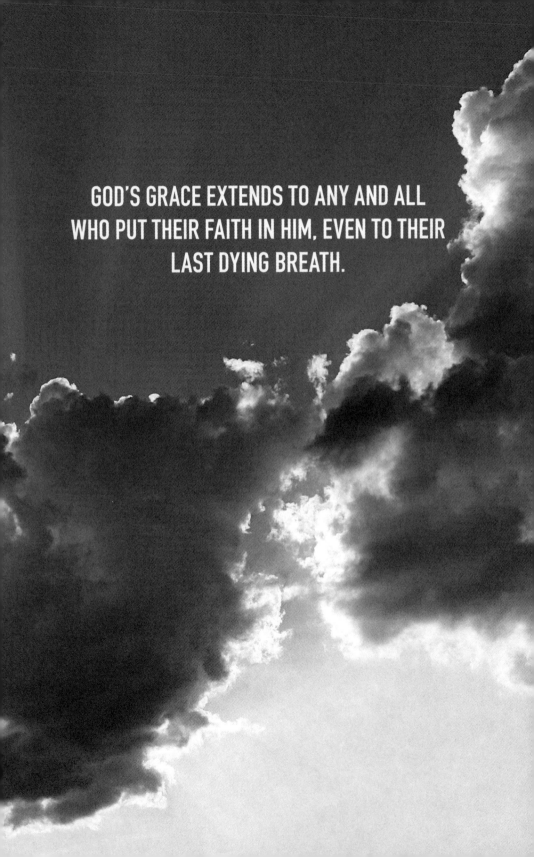

GOD'S GRACE EXTENDS TO ANY AND ALL
WHO PUT THEIR FAITH IN HIM, EVEN TO THEIR
LAST DYING BREATH.

the earth?" (Revelation 6:10). Even in the current heavenly realms, there is still a longing for that promised Day of the Lord.

John was captivated by a vision there of a great multitude that had washed their robes in the blood of the Lamb. It is their joy and delight to praise the Lord all the rest of eternity. John is told of this great multitude:

> *They shall hunger no more, neither thirst anymore;*
> *the sun shall not strike them,*
> *nor any scorching heat.*
> *For the Lamb in the midst of the throne will be their shepherd,*
> *and he will guide them to springs of living water,*
> *and God will wipe away every tear from their eyes.*
>
> **Revelation 7:16-17**

For those who have died and live in Heaven, the tribulation of this life is over. Those who have finished the race and won the prize of faithful endurance are healed and restored, and they, too, await the New Heavens and New Earth. And they worship in glorious and joyous splendor in the presence of King Jesus, the Lamb who was slain.

REFLECT:

When you think about the New Heavens and the New Earth, what do you imagine? What are you looking forward to in that day? The Scripture tells us that Jesus will one day dwell bodily in our midst. But for now, He dwells in our hearts. How often do you sense His presence there? Why not take a moment to ask Him to make His presence more real in your daily life.

_____

_____

_____

_____

_____

_____

_____

_____

_____

WEEK THREE
THE THIRD WORD
RELATIONSHIP

"WOMAN, BEHOLD, YOUR SON!...BEHOLD, YOUR MOTHER!"

When the soldiers had crucified Jesus, they took his garments and divided them into four parts, one part for each soldier; also his tunic. But the tunic was seamless, woven in one piece from top to bottom, so they said to one another, "Let us not tear it, but cast lots for it to see whose it shall be." This was to fulfill the Scripture, which says,

"They divided my garments among them,
and for my clothing they cast lots."

So the soldiers did these things, but standing by the cross of Jesus were his mother and his mother's sister, Mary the wife of Clopas, and Mary Magdalene. When Jesus saw his mother and the disciple whom he loved standing nearby, he said to his mother, "Woman, behold, your son!" Then he said to the disciple, "Behold, your mother!" And from that hour the disciple took her to his own home. **John 19:23-27**

DAY 12
SUNDAY
THE SEEDS OF A NEW FAMILY

"Woman, behold, your son!...Behold, your mother!"

On one level, the exchange, *"Woman, behold, your son!...Behold, your mother!"* is simply a matter of Jesus ministering to two people He loved. In His hour of crucifixion, He showed deep care and compassion for His mother and His disciple John, even while He suffered not only physical, but also spiritual distress, as He bore the sins of the entire world in His body.

Who were these two individuals whom Jesus loved so dearly that He spoke to them directly from the cross?

His mother, Mary, was visited by the angel Gabriel as a young virgin and chosen by God to be blessed among women for bearing the Son of God. When Jesus was born, Mary delighted in her son. She treasured in her heart the words the angels had spoken about Him as told to her by the visiting shepherds. And after the prophet Simeon announced the glory of the baby Jesus, the Scripture reads, *"And his father and his mother marveled at what was said about him"* (Luke 2:33).

Yet for all Mary's joy and marvel about her son, this mother was prophetically warned that her heart would eventually be pierced:

And Simeon blessed them and said to Mary his mother, "Behold, this child is appointed for the fall and rising of many in Israel, and for a sign that is opposed (and a sword will pierce through your own soul also), so that thoughts from many hearts may be revealed."   **Luke 2:34-35**

As Jesus' mother, Mary had a special place in His heart, so much so that He submitted to her untimely urging to intervene during a wedding in Cana of Galilee by turning water into wine (John 2:1-11). Jesus loved His mother.

Likewise, Jesus held a deep love for the youngest of the disciples, John, who did not flee with the other twelve, did not betray Him, did not deny Him, but stood steadfast with Jesus all the way to the foot of the cross. John was dear to the heart of Jesus as the one who reclined next to Him at the Last Supper before His agonizing journey. In his Gospel, John refers to himself as the disciple whom Jesus loved. John was the only one of the twelve disciples who would not be martyred for the faith but live to a very ripe age and eventually die as an old man in exile on Patmos Island.

While, on the one hand, Jesus' words to Mary and John, *"Woman, behold your son,"* and *"Son, behold your mother,"* were a gesture of care and protection for those He loved, they were also the beginning of a new reality that came into existence with His death on the cross. Jesus was inaugurating a new family!

Mary and John were the seeds of the new family of God. They would be the first two members of an extended family of spiritual mothers and fathers, brothers and sisters, who share a common patrimony and family relationship as adopted sons and daughters of God. Under one Father, they are united, not by flesh, but by the unifying Spirit of Jesus Christ who will live in them.

If you are in Christ, your new family was born at the foot of the cross. Jesus' gift to John and Mary is the same gift He offers you—a new start in the family of God.

REFLECT:

Where have you experienced a sense of family among God's people? Who has been a spiritual father or mother to you? Who would you consider your closest brother or sister in Christ? If you do not yet feel truly connected to the family of God, ask God to help you and to bring you close brothers and sisters in Christ.

_____

_____

_____

_____

_____

_____

_____

_____

_____

DAY 13
MONDAY
THE TIES THAT BIND

Yesterday, we talked about the beginning of a new family—the family of God—that Jesus inaugurated at the cross, by speaking these words to His mother, Mary, and His disciple John: *"Woman, behold your son!"* and *"Son, behold your mother!"* At the cross, there is a launching of a new spiritual family that will supersede our natural families.

We were given hints of this reality earlier in Jesus' ministry:

While he was still speaking to the people, behold, his mother and his brothers stood outside, asking to speak to him. But he replied to the man who told him, "Who is my mother, and who are my brothers?"

And stretching out his hand toward his disciples, he said, "Here are my mother and my brothers! For whoever does the will of my Father in heaven is my brother and sister and mother."

Matthew 12:46-50

Sometimes, our family of birth is one of our main problems.

Many of us have had the experience of realizing at some point in our lives—it happened to me when I was in my 20s—that we display many of the character traits that we do not like in our fathers and mothers. Has that ever happened to you? The very things that most frustrate you about your natural parents, you yourself do. "Oh no!" you say to yourself, "I'm reacting just like my father would." Or, "I sound just like my mother!"

The Bible teaches that sins of our parents are passed down generationally. But the good news is, through the cross and resurrection of Jesus, those cycles of repeating patterns of sin can be broken and laid to rest, never to rear their ugly heads again.

It's actually stronger than that. Not only can those ties that bind be broken, they must be broken. If we are to be truly liberated, we must be freed from the inheritance of the flesh passed down from our natural families, beginning with Adam.

All of us are in Adam—guilty of the sin of our first parents, heirs of an inheritance of guilt, shame, death, condemnation, and eternal judgment.

Paul reveals in 1 Corinthians:

For as by a man came death, by a man has come also the resurrection of the dead. For as in Adam all die, so also in Christ shall all be made alive.   **1 Corinthians 15:21-22**

Our birthright inherited from our natural parents is death. And if we claim that birthright, we will surely die. If we find our identity only in our earthly family, we will remain separate and separated from the family of God.

This does not mean that we should neglect our natural families. On the contrary, we are told to love and provide for them. Jesus provided for his natural mother, Mary, at the foot of the cross. The Apostle Paul writes to Timothy, *"But if anyone does not provide for his relatives, and especially for members of his household, he has denied the faith and is worse than an unbeliever"* (1 Timothy 5:8).

Our family of origin may bless us with patterns of obedience and faithfulness to God over generations. For this, we can praise God and claim that faithfulness for ourselves and our children! However, when we see patterns of sin and destruction, we need to die to those influences and bring them to the foot of the cross. They are a direct inheritance from Adam's disobedience, passed through our natural families.

Our new family—the family of God—gives us an inheritance that is nothing less than eternal life.

REFLECT:

Do you see the ties to Adam's disobedience in your own family of origin? Where have those ties to Adam manifested in your own life? Have you received spiritual blessings from those who were faithful to God in your natural family? How so?

_____

_____

_____

_____

_____

_____

_____

_____

_____

_____

_____

DAY 14
TUESDAY
BREAKING THE TIES

There are times in our lives when we have to break certain ties with our natural families. I had to do this when I was in college, after I surrendered my life to the Lord.

At that time, my father had selected a specific path for me to walk in life. He wanted me to go into business with him. I seriously considered it. I had worked with him for many years. But deep inside, I knew God's call on my life would take a different direction. My earthly father's path for me was not the path of the Heavenly Father.

Looking back, I believe the best thing to do in a situation like this is to pray that your parent, or whoever stands in the way of the path you believe God has for you, would change their heart and mind. Then allow time for that to happen. Consider it a blessing if your parents are believers. They will be more open to the leading of the Holy Spirit as you pray. However, at times, family members will remain fixed to their plan rather than the one you believe God has for you. This is what happened to me.

I remember having to think and pray through what might happen if my decision resulted in my losing my relationship with my parents. One of the hardest things I've ever had to do was to go to my father and say, "Dad, the family business that you have been preparing for me, what a wonderful gift! But I am going to walk a different path."

Before talking with my father, I remember being struck by the passage of Scripture that talked about counting the cost of being a disciple of Jesus. And it says,

If anyone comes to me and does not hate his own father and mother and wife and children and brothers and sisters, yes, and even his own life, he cannot be my disciple. Whoever does not bear his own cross and come after me cannot be my disciple.
Luke 14:26-27

When I first read that passage, I remember thinking to myself, "Wow, that is such strong language! Why would Jesus say that?"

But after my experience, I understood the passage in a different way. It is not that I literally had to hate my father. Rather, as a mature believer, I had to make a break and, in a sense, die to what my earthly father had prepared for me so that I could receive what my Heavenly Father had called me to do. In that moment, I purposed to be a person who picked up my cross and followed Jesus, no matter what the cost.

CONSIDER IT A BLESSING IF YOUR PARENTS ARE BELIEVERS. THEY WILL BE MORE OPEN TO THE LEADING OF THE HOLY SPIRIT AS YOU PRAY.

Thankfully, my relationship with my earthly father is stronger than ever, but we have a very different relationship. Our relationship is no longer founded on the natural level. On the contrary, it is a spiritual relationship. We are freed from each other's earthly expectations in a way that can happen only through dying to self and dying to the natural family while being united to your new family and your new identity.

REFLECT:

Do you find your primary identity in your family of flesh or your spiritual family? Breaking the ties of your natural family can be done only through the power of God. Ask Him to show you any of the earthly ties that bind you to a path that is not His path. He desires to free you completely that He might present you to your new spiritual family. This family is a gift from Jesus.

_____

_____

_____

_____

_____

_____

_____

_____

_____

DAY 15
WEDNESDAY
BURY THE HATCHET

We've all heard of the famous Hatfields and McCoys, the iconic feuding families of West Virginia and Kentucky. Consider that almost every war on this planet ultimately goes back to identity found in family of origin. For example, the clash between the Muslim Arabs and the Jewish people goes back to their ancestors, Ishmael and Isaac. The fighting in Ireland between Roman Catholics and Protestants stems more directly from tribal and family feuds than anything pertaining to the Christian faith.

When humans go to war, it is often because they find their identities in their natural families or human ancestry. Family divides people into factions and parties. The worst factions of any on earth are factions in and among families.

Blood is thicker than anything else, and bad blood is more dangerous than anything else. It is what often separates Caucasians from African-Americans, Greeks from Turks, Jews from non-Jews and fuels countless other divisions around the world.

God is calling believers to be one family under one head, to share one Lord, one baptism, one Spirit. To fulfill that call, we must die, in a sense, to our families of origin and to our "tribes," so that we can be raised up into the restored family of Christ Jesus our Lord.

Now those are strong words. Here is an interesting phrase we sometimes use: "Bury the hatchet." The origin of the phrase is uniquely American; it is derived from the Native Americans. When a tribe would come to a point of declaring peace with another tribe, they would literally dig a hole and bury their weapons of war in the ground, thus burying the bloody hatchet for the cause of peace.

Listen to how Paul describes a similar feat accomplished on the cross:

But now in Christ Jesus you who once were far off have been brought near by the blood of Christ. For he himself is our peace, who has made us both one and has broken down in his flesh the dividing wall of hostility by abolishing the law of commandments expressed in ordinances, that he might create in himself one new man in place of the two, so making peace, and might reconcile us both to God in one body through the cross, thereby killing the hostility.
Ephesians 2:13-16

Now, Paul was originally speaking of Jews and non-Jews (Gentiles). God's plan is not that there should be separate Jewish and Gentile tribes divided by ethnicities and patrimonies, but that there should be one new man from the two, in Jesus Christ, where the dividing wall of hostility is abolished in His flesh. The two sides bury the bloody hatchet at the foot of the cross—creating peace between them.

And he came and preached peace to you who were far off and peace to those who were near. For through him we both have access in one Spirit to the Father. **Ephesians 2:17-18**

When Jesus said to John and to Mary, "*Woman, behold your son… behold your mother,*" Jesus began an incredible peace process between all families, tribes, and nations by starting this new family of God. In Jesus, people are united by common faith and spiritual adoption rather than by blood. John writes of this new family: *"But to all who did receive him, who believed in his name, He gave the right to become children of God, who were born, not of blood nor of the will of the flesh nor of the will of man, but of God"* (John 1:12-13).

REFLECT:

I ask you, do you carry a hatchet in your hand directed toward any other? Is there any form of enmity or strife in your life caused by relational ties to any earthly identity or relationship? How does the reconciliation of the Gospel apply? The dividing walls of hostility cannot stand at the foot of the cross. God calls you to peace; it is time to bury the bloody hatchet at the foot of the cross.

_____

_____

_____

_____

_____

_____

_____

_____

_____

DAY 16
THURSDAY
GRIEVING OUR OLD FAMILY

Whenever you grieve the loss of your old family, you have to go through a process that has been observed as the stages of grief. The process includes denial, anger, bargaining, depression, and ultimately acceptance. That acceptance brings us to peace.

But to get there, you have to grieve. You have to walk the mourner's path. And I believe that John and Mary were given to each other because they were going to need one another to walk that mourner's path. Just three days from the day Jesus spoke to them from the cross, Mary and John would see Jesus again as the resurrected Christ.

From that point on, life was changed. He was the risen Lord Jesus Christ. He was the Lord of the Cosmos. Mary and John had to accept the new reality.

Psychotherapist and author Miriam Greenspan describes grief this way: "Grief, fear, and despair are the emotions we humans find most disturbing, and they are the most likely to get us into trouble when we ignore them. I call them dark emotions, not because they're negative but because they're painful and because our culture tends to shame, silence, devalue, and deny them." [1]

These are the very mental processes that we must go through if we pick up our cross and follow Jesus.

A significant portion of the grieving we go through in life is because of the loss through death of one we care about. When we lose someone close to us, we often feel as though we have lost a part of who we are. We suddenly feel as though we will never again be the person we once were. It is often the perceived death of part of who we are that is so difficult to accept.

At the foot of the cross, Mary and John lost the earthly relationship they had with Jesus. With that loss, they may have felt they also lost a portion of themselves. Mary's heart was pierced. She would never again be able to relate to Jesus as her earthly son. John would never again be able to relate to Him simply as a young son would to an earthly father. The old would give way to a new Resurrection reality. Their relationship with Jesus would no longer stem from a fleshly point of view.

Paul aptly puts it this way: From now on, therefore, we regard no one according to the flesh. Even though we once regarded Christ according to the flesh, we regard him thus no longer (2 Cor. 5:16). Paul then spells out the implication of the change for individual believers—for those who have gone through the conversion of the cross:

Therefore, if anyone is in Christ, he is a new creation. The old has passed away; behold, the new has come.   **2 Corinthians 5:17**

Just as we have to grieve the old family, we are called to grieve the old self. Our identities are no longer to be found in our natural inheritance. The loss is significant and real, the old is gone, the new has come. We regard no one according to the flesh—including our old self.

We are frightened to become who we are about to become because we do not know how to be that new person. And without realizing it, we still may grieve for the old self. That unfinished grief can make life in the new self less than fulfilling. So grieve we must!

REFLECT:

We grieve our old family and our old self so that we might live for Christ and for our new family. What aspects of your old self are you having a difficult time letting go?

_____

_____

_____

_____

_____

_____

_____

_____

_____

DAY 17
FRIDAY
BAPTISM AND THE CROSS

Whenever someone is baptized, he or she is baptized into the cross of Jesus Christ and raised, as signified by the water, into life as a new person, a new creation.

Do you remember when Jesus was approached at night by Nicodemus and asked, *"Teacher, what must I do to inherit eternal life?"* What was Jesus' response? He said, *"You must be born again."* Nicodemus wondered, *"How can I go back into my mother's womb?"* And Jesus chided him: *"Nicodemus, you are a teacher of the law. You should know what the Scripture teaches."*

You don't go back into your mother's womb. No, instead you must be born of the Spirit. Flesh gives birth to flesh, but spirit gives birth to spirit.

You must become a new person, and become part of a new family. The cross serves as both the ending point and the starting point; it is the ending point of the old family and the beginning point of the new family.

"Woman, behold your son!" And then to John, *"Behold your Mother!"*

The Sacrament of Baptism therefore conveys both the reality of the crucifixion (dying to the old self) and the reality of the resurrection (new birth into a new family).

First, baptism is the sacramental action of co-crucifixion with Jesus. The mode of full immersion is best for conveying this tangibly:

Do you not know that all of us who have been baptized into Christ Jesus were baptized into his death? We were buried therefore with him by baptism into death, in order that, just as Christ was raised from the dead by the glory of the Father, we too might walk in newness of life.
Romans 6:3-4

When a new believer is taken under the water, he or she is mysteriously buried with Christ in His death. When they emerge from the water, they are raised with Christ in the new life of the resurrection.

Baptism is also the sign that points to the new family. Whenever infants or new believers are presented to the family of God for baptism, they are presented with their first and middle names only. Our first name is traditionally called our Christian name. Our last name is called our family name. When a new member is presented to the congregation, we will leave off his family of origin name. This is because, no matter which earthly family he or she belongs to, the newly baptized person is also getting a new family, the family of God, and is being adopted as a spiritual child of God.

THE CROSS SERVES AS BOTH THE ENDING POINT AND THE STARTING POINT.

After a person is baptized, the priest says the words and marks a Sign of the Cross on the candidate's forehead: *"You are sealed by the Holy Spirit in Baptism and marked as Christ's own forever."*

Holy Baptism, Book of Common Prayer

The new family then welcomes its newest members with these words: *"We receive you into the household of God. Confess the faith of Christ crucified, proclaim His resurrection, and share with us in His eternal priesthood"* (Book of Common Prayer).

In other words, "Welcome to the family!"

REFLECT:

Think about your own baptism. Let those words sink into your mind and heart. You have been buried with Christ in His death. You have been raised with Christ in His resurrection to a new life in Him. You are sealed by the Holy Spirit in Baptism and marked as Christ's own forever. Welcome to the family!

_____

_____

_____

_____

_____

_____

_____

_____

_____

DAY 18
SATURDAY
THE GIFT OF ONE ANOTHER

Jesus gives John to Mary and Mary to John, and it is the gift of the new. It is the gift of one another. Do you know that in the New Testament there are over 40 "one another" statements? We are told in the book of Hebrews:

And let us consider how to stir up one another to love and good works, not neglecting to meet together, as is the habit of some, but encouraging one another, and all the more as you see the Day draw-ing near.   **Hebrews 10:24-25**

Think about how those words might apply to John and Mary. They should not give up meeting together. They should not isolate themselves in this dreadful moment of Jesus' death, but, rather, they should spur one another on towards love and good deeds. Following the crucifixion, all of Jesus' disciples would need each other in order to face the unknown. They should mutually encour-age one another, literally "to breathe courage" into one another as they face very fearful days ahead. Mary and John were Jesus' gift to one another just as the new family of God is God's gift to you—the gift of one another.

I am going to give you a rapid-fire list of all the "one another" statements from the New Testament. Allow these encouragements to spur you on to deeper fellowship in the family of God, to become a type of blueprint for relationships.

- Be at peace with one another (Mark 9:50).

- Wash one another's feet (John 13:14).

- Love one another: just as I have loved you, you also are to love one another (John 13:34, see also 13:35; 15:12, 17).

- Love one another with brotherly affection (Romans 12:10a).

- Outdo one another in showing honor (Romans 12:10b).

- Live in harmony with one another (Romans 12:16).

- Welcome one another as Christ has welcomed you, for the glory of God (Romans 15:7).

- Greet one another with a holy kiss (Romans 16:16).

- Wait for one another (1 Corinthians 11:33).

- Have the same care for one another (1 Corinthians 12:25).

- Aim for restoration, comfort one another, agree with one other, live in peace (2 Corinthians 13:11).

- Through love, serve one another (Galatians 5:13).

- Bear one another's burdens (Galatians 6:2).

- Bear with one another in love (Ephesians 4:2).

- Be kind to one another, tenderhearted (Ephesians 4:32a).

- Forgive one another, as God in Christ forgave you (Ephesians 4:32b).

- Paul exhorts us to be filled with the Spirit by:

  - addressing one another in psalms and hymns and spiritual songs (Ephesians 5:19).

  - submitting to one another out of reverence for Christ (Ephesians 5:21).

- Bear with one another (Colossians 3:13a).

- If one has a complaint against another, forgive each other (Colossians 3:13b).

- Let the word of Christ dwell in you richly, teaching and admonishing one another in all wisdom, singing psalms and hymns and spiritual songs, with thankfulness in your hearts to God (Colossians 3:16).

- May the Lord make you increase and abound in love for one another (1 Thessalonians 3:12).

- Encourage one another with these words (1 Thessalonians 4:18).

- Encourage one another and build one another up, just as you are doing (1 Thessalonians 5:11).

- Always seek to do good to one another (1 Thessalonians 5:15).

- Exhort one another every day (Hebrews 3:13).

- Let us consider how to stir up one another to love and good works (Hebrews 10:24).

- Not neglecting to meet together, as is the habit of some, but encouraging one another (Hebrews 10:25).

- Confess your sins to one another and pray for one another, that you may be healed (James 5:16).

By far, the most repeated encouragement in the New Testament is to love one another. Peter encourages us to *"love one another earnestly from a pure heart"* (1 Peter 1:22); and again he says, *"keep loving one another earnestly, since love covers a multitude of sins"* (1 Peter 4:8). There are a total of six "love one another" admonitions in John's letters (1 John 3:11, 23; 4:7, 11, 12; 2 John 1:5).

Love one another.

- Show hospitality to one another without grumbling (1 Peter 4:9).

- As each has received a gift, use it to serve one another, as good stewards of God's varied grace (1 Peter 4:10).

- Clothe yourselves, all of you, with humility toward one another (1 Peter 5:5).

- Greet one another with the kiss of love (1 Peter 5:14).

And then we have the five commands of "do not" do.

- Let us not pass judgment on one another (Romans 14:13).

- Let us not become conceited, provoking one another, envying one another (Galatians 5:26).

- Do not lie to one another (Colossians 3:9).

- Do not speak evil against one another (James 4:11).

- Do not grumble against one another (James 5:9).

REFLECT:

Jesus has given us to one another as a gift to be treasured, stewarded, guarded, and loved. Which of the "one another" statements from the Scriptures spoke to your heart today? How can you apply that practice to your relationships today?

_____

_____

_____

_____

_____

_____

_____

_____

_____

WEEK FOUR
THE FOURTH WORD
DISTRESS

"I THIRST."

    After this, Jesus, knowing that all was now fin-
ished, said (to fulfill the Scripture), "I thirst."
    A jar full of sour wine stood there, so they put
a sponge full of the sour wine on a hyssop branch
and held it to his mouth. **John 19:28-29**

DAY 19
SUNDAY
WATER IN THE WILDERNESS

"...I will not be mastered by anything."
　　　　　—The Apostle Paul, **1 Corinthians 6:12 (NIV)**

The archetypical representation of worldly power, protection, and provision in the Old Testament is Egypt. As we read in the book of Genesis, on more than one occasion the people of God fled famine and foreign enemies into the provident hands of the Egyptian pharaohs and the Egyptian people. The first to do this was the great patriarch Abraham.

Genesis reads: *"Now there was a famine in the land, and Abram went down to Egypt to live there for a while because the famine was severe"* (Genesis 12:10). Several generations later, twelve of Abraham's great-grandchildren would follow in his footsteps as they also looked to Egypt for provision during a time of famine.

The problem with seeking refuge in Egypt was the cost. You may enter as God's free people, but not stay that way for long. There was a price to be paid. Egypt demanded the self-sacrifice of your freedom and the sacrifice of your wife and children. For four hundred years, many generations of the people of God toiled under the tyrannical burden of bondage to their Egyptian protectors and providers. Worldly powers are like that; they promise protection and provision, but always at the cost of human freedom and dignity.

God would have his people be free and dependent on Him alone. Following the great salvation of Israel from Egypt, God led the people into a season of wilderness wandering. While in their minds they all desired to be free from the bondage of Egypt, their hearts had been shaped by a slave-like dependency on Egyptian provision. The Lord used the distress of forty years of wilderness wandering to purge this Egyptian dependency out of Israel.

Again and again, the people grumbled against the leadership of Moses as he led them through the barren landscape of the desert wilderness:

[They] . . . camped at Rephidim, but there was no water for the people to drink. So they quarreled with Moses and said, "Give us water to drink."

Moses replied, "Why do you quarrel with me? Why do you put the LORD to the test?"

But the people were thirsty for water there, and they grumbled against Moses. They said, "Why did you bring us up out of Egypt to make us and our children and livestock die of thirst?"

Exodus 17:1-3

Yet in their thirst, they learned a very important lesson. God would teach the Israelites that He was to be their provider. Again and again, the Lord provided food, water, and protection for the people as they cried out for His provision. When their slavery-formed hearts looked back nostalgically at the provision of Egypt, God disciplined them until they cried out to Him alone for salvation and sustenance.

The LORD answered Moses, "Go out in front of the people. Take with you some of the elders of Israel and take in your hand the staff with which you struck the Nile, and go. I will stand there before you by the rock at Horeb. Strike the rock, and water will come out of it for the people to drink." So Moses did this in the sight of the elders of Israel. And he called the place Massah and Meribah because the Israelites quarreled and because they tested the LORD saying, "Is the LORD among us or not?"

Exodus 17:5-7

The Hebrew name Massah means "testing." The Israelites "tested" the Lord by their mistrust and doubt of His provision and nostalgic longing for Egyptian worldly provision. The Lord would have them simply trust Him. The Hebrew name Meribah means "quarreling." They had argued, "Is the Lord among us or not?"

The history of humanity demonstrates that human beings continually test and quarrel with God. We so often find it extremely difficult to trust and submit to His provision. We grow impatient with His timing and methods of providing. Sadly, testing and quarrelling with the Lord can thrust us straight into the promising arms of worldly refuge and provision.

Have you ever asked, "Is the Lord with me or not?" The question is exactly backwards. You should ask yourself, "Am I with the Lord or not?"

So often, when we find ourselves in seasons of distress, we test God and quarrel with him for not partnering with us to fulfill our agenda and our will for our lives. God does desire to provide water for His people, but the goal of our journey is to trust and look to Him for His leading and guidance.

When Jesus cried, "I thirst" from the cross, He expressed distress. But it was not the first time He had experienced human distress. At the beginning of His ministry, Jesus, too, was led into the wilderness for forty days. In that place of desolation, He showed us the way to handle distress. In response to the temptations that came to Him, He demonstrated total faith:

"It is written: 'Man shall not live by bread alone, but by every word that comes from the mouth of God.' "   **Matthew 4:4**

In His flesh, every fiber of Jesus' being would cry out for physical bread (Satan's offer), but Jesus had a complete and total trust in the Father's good provision in the time of need. The bread that comes from the mouth of God is the spiritual food of God's Word. Earthly bread feeds the body for only a moment; the Word feeds the soul for all eternity. Many people have forfeited their souls for a slice of earthly bread. Jesus shows us the way to hunger for the food that truly is life.

REFLECT:

Are you experiencing a time of wilderness? How can the struggles of Israel and the example of Jesus help you? In what ways do you look to the world rather than to the Lord for provision? Allow the distress of these present trials to lead you to a total dependence on God.

_____

_____

_____

_____

_____

_____

_____

_____

_____

DAY 20
MONDAY
THE CHOICE TO SUFFER

"I thirst" is the shortest of the seven last words. In fact, it is only one word in Greek, the word διψω, which is pronounced dip-sō.

After this, Jesus, knowing that all was now finished, said (to fulfill the Scripture), *"I thirst."*   **John 19:28**

The distress of the cross did not catch Jesus off guard. Jesus was fully in control and knew exactly what He was doing. He was purposeful in His actions. Jesus' purpose was to complete the task, to persevere to the very end, to finish the work that the Lord, His God and Father, had given Him to do. It was a work that is found in the pages of Holy Scripture itself: the call to be the suffering servant.

One of the questions that arise is, why would anyone purpose to suffer distress? Indeed, the very idea is foreign to the ears of people in our time and culture. We work so incredibly hard to avoid and minimize distress in our lives. Indeed, avoiding distress has become an all-consuming goal of Americans. Pat Morley in his book The Man in the Mirror sums up that goal in what he describes as the "wrinkle-free life."

The wrinkle-free life is one in which we minimize pain, avoid suffering, age without stress, and retire in comfort. Unfortunately, the more focused our culture becomes on pursuing this self-serving wrinkle-free life, the more surprised we are by the stress-filled lives we have created for ourselves.

The Lord has a word to such a cultural pursuit:

Now, therefore, thus says the LORD of hosts: Consider your ways. You have sown much, and harvested little. You eat, but you never have enough; you drink, but you never have your fill. You clothe yourselves, but no one is warm. And he who earns wages does so to put them into a bag with holes.   **Haggai 1:5-6**

The more we pursue the "wrinkle-free life," the more it seems to elude us. Perhaps the goal is wrong. Indeed, it is dead wrong. Paul writes of those who pursue the prevailing lifestyle of the world:

For many, of whom I have often told you and now tell you even with tears, walk as enemies of the cross of Christ. Their end is destruction, their god is their belly, and they glory in their shame, with minds set on earthly things.

Philippians 3:18-19

Jesus calls us to pick up our cross and follow Him. That does not sound like the easy, stress-free, painless path the world celebrates. On the contrary, the Lord is inviting us to join Him in *"sharing in his sufferings"* (Philippians 3:10).

WE WORK SO INCREDIBLY HARD TO AVOID AND MINIMIZE DISTRESS IN OUR LIVES.

The followers of Christ must willingly suffer and endure when called to do so. We are not to seek out suffering and thereby become self-proclaimed martyrs. But this is a sinful and fallen world. In order to be on the side of righteousness and truth, grace and love, we will undoubtedly experience opposition from evil powers and people. The world will marshal its forces against us. If the world persecuted Christ, it will persecute His followers. We should expect nothing less.

One of the ways to prepare for these moments of trial is to intentionally enter periods of self-denial as a way of steeling ourselves. Faithful Christians have long recognized the spiritual disciplines as useful for strengthening the character of our hearts and the resolve of our spirits.

Christian disciplines of self-denial include fasting from something that we enjoy, giving away money to the poor, keeping Sabbath worship, or sacrificing our time in service to others and to the Church. While the fleshly nature is naturally lazy and seeks to avoid pain and hard work, the spiritual disciplines help check our self-centered focus and rein in our desires. By engaging in the disciplines of self-denial in times of blessing and plenty, we help build the necessary fortitude to face the inevitable times of trial.

Pastor John Piper called fasting "The Hungry Handmaiden of Faith." Fasting, as well as almsgiving, service, and other forms of self-sacrifice, serves us in our faith journey by revealing to us our weakness in the flesh and showing us the strength of character God wants to build in us.

REFLECT:

During this season of Lent, how are you engaging in the disciplines of self-denial? Where do you see God addressing the damaging forces of self-centeredness in your own life? In what ways have you been shaped by the world's pursuit of the "wrinkle-free life"? In what ways is Christ shaping you into the character of the cross?

_____

_____

_____

_____

_____

_____

_____

_____

_____

_____

DAY 21
TUESDAY
FULFILLMENT OF SCRIPTURES

There are two specific passages in the Old Testament Scriptures that relate to Jesus' cry on the cross, "I thirst."

The first is Psalm 22. This Psalm begins with one of the other seven last words from the cross: *"My God, my God, why have you forsaken me?"*

These words are a lament written by King David 1,000 years before the crucifixion of Jesus Christ. Further into the Psalm, in verse 16, we find a precise description of crucifixion: "They have pierced my hands and feet." The Psalm also describes the dividing up and casting lots for His clothing (soldiers cast lots for Jesus' garments at the cross). Finally, for our focus, verses 14 & 15 prophetically read:

> *I am poured out like water,*
> *and all my bones are out of joint;*
> *my heart is like wax;*
> *it is melted within my breast;*
> *my strength is dried up like a potsherd,*
> *and my tongue sticks to my jaws;*
> *you lay me in the dust of death.*

"My tongue sticks to my jaws," is a graphic image of intense thirst. Scholars believe Psalm 22 foreshadows the suffering of Jesus on the cross, including his severe thirst.

There is a second passage that foreshadows the passion of Jesus on the cross. (Perhaps Jesus had this one in mind as well.) Psalm 69:21 (NIV) reads, *"They put gall in my food and gave me vinegar for my thirst."* This passage is almost a direct parallel to John's account of Jesus at Calvary:

A jar full of sour wine stood there, so they put a sponge full of the sour wine on a hyssop branch and held it to his mouth. **John 19:29**

These Old Testament passages predict what would happen to the Messiah, Jesus. We call such predictions prophecy.

Jesus was keenly aware of these prophecies. He knew that every single thing He was doing or undergoing fulfilled one Scripture passage or another. Every moment, every word spoken was an intentional submission to the Word of God. Nothing was out of Jesus' control.

Some would try to claim responsibility and therefore power over Jesus—Judas, for example, as he led the guard to arrest Jesus in the Garden of Gethsemane—but Jesus responded to the arrest saying, *"Let the Scriptures be fulfilled."* (Mark 14:49).

John records Pilate saying to Jesus, *"Don't you know I have the power to free you?"* Jesus replies, *"You would have no authority over me unless it had been given you from above."* In other words, God placed Pilate in his position of authority in order that he would have the power to order Jesus' crucifixion.

Jesus perfectly fulfilled the Scriptures in His life. He completely and faithfully fulfilled all the Old Testament laws in His life and in death so that He might establish the promise of His covenant. Details about His birth, life, death by crucifixion, and resurrection were prophesized in the Scriptures hundreds of years before He was ever born.

All of our lives, too, are to be ordered in accordance with the teaching of the Scriptures. If we are to be a people who follow the Son of God, who gave up His life for us, if we are to be His disciples, we must fulfill the Scriptures. We do this through the daily choices we make in our lives by the power of the Holy Spirit, including what we give up for the sake of Jesus' Way found in the Scriptures.

Not all of the things written in the Scriptures are easy to apply to our lives. Some Scriptures challenge us to avoid behaviors and attitudes that our culture embraces and permits. The Apostle Paul writes, *"All things are lawful for me…but not all things are helpful"* (1 Cor. 6:12). In other words, even if something is not strictly forbidden in Scripture, we have to ask ourselves if it is truly beneficial or uplifting for us and for those around us.

The Scriptures call us to a higher ethical standard than we would ever call ourselves. Jesus addressed the cultural standards of His day by saying: "You have heard that it is said…but I say…." In other words, Jesus maintained that His standards were above and beyond what "you have heard" in the culture or the law of the land. The laws and standards of society never call us to the high standard of the character of Christ. Our righteousness must exceed that of the Scribes (teachers of the law) and Pharisees. And when we have the fruit of the Spirit in our lives, we go far and above the requirements of the law.

But personal sacrifice is often required to fulfill and obey the teaching of the Scripture, to yield to the Holy Spirit's fruit in our lives rather than to our fleshly desires. Jesus shows us the way when He calls out: *I thirst.*

Jesus chose to endure intense suffering, including extreme thirst akin to total dehydration, in order to fulfill the Scriptures. He would "drink the cup that the Father had given him"—a cup filled with all of the sin and degradation of the human race—in order to purchase our forgiveness and salvation. His purpose was to accomplish the Father's will, no matter what it entailed. Jesus hungered and thirsted for righteousness. He submitted His life obediently to the upward call of God the Father as it was revealed in the Holy Scriptures.

REFLECT:

Is your singular desire to yield your life to the call of God the Father as revealed to you in the Holy Scriptures? Or are you holding back? What is preventing you from truly giving in to a deep spiritual thirst for God's will?

_____

_____

_____

_____

_____

_____

_____

_____

_____

DAY 22
WEDNESDAY
THE REALITY OF HUMAN SUFFERING

The saying *"I thirst"* reveals the physical suffering that Jesus underwent as a human being.

One powerful prophecy in the Old Testament (Isaiah 53) describes the coming Messiah as a suffering servant. Isaiah 53:3a says, *"He was despised and rejected by men, a man of sorrows, and familiar with suffering"* (NIV).

By suffering death through crucifixion, Jesus underwent one of the most intense forms of torture that human beings have ever conjured up to inflict upon one another. Nothing is more painful or more agonizing or more prolonged than the suffering of death by crucifixion.

Some have speculated that the wine mixed with myrrh that the Roman soldier offered to Jesus on the cross was the kind offer of a sedative to dull the pain. Other interpreters see it as a bitter and mocking gesture to actually compound His thirst with sour wine. Regardless, the saying "I thirst" and what followed with the offer of gall reveals that Jesus underwent deep distress and suffering.

Jesus was fully a human being. He understood what it feels like to be in pain, to be hungry, to have your friends betray you, to have your friends deny you, to be carried off by a perversion of justice. He understood what it feels like to be tortured, to be mocked, to be spit on.

I thirst.

Jesus still understands what it feels like to be sick and to suffer and experience pain. He was a man of sorrows and familiar with sufferings.

In this life on earth, we certainly experience sufferings. People sin against us. Confidantes say things that hurt us. Intimate and close friends betray us.

Sometimes others hurt us intentionally, out of spite or a sinful and evil heart. At other times, our loved ones wound us without intending us harm, because they, too, are wounded and live as finite human beings. Sometimes we suffer and we hurt. We grieve the loss of our friends. We grieve the loss of control of our bodies. We suffer, at times, even to the point of death. Jesus bore our sufferings. Isaiah says, *"Surely he has borne our griefs..."* (Isaiah 53:4a NIV 1984).

There's nothing you can go through in this life that Jesus has not gone through and will not go through with you. You may be in the midst of a challenging time in your life, in the midst of a time of suffering, of pain, of hurt, either at the hands of another person or because your body is falling apart. Perhaps it is for some other reason, such as injustice. Whatever your pain or suffering, Jesus understands! He has been there before you, and He is with you now.

The writer of Hebrews describes Jesus as a high priest, but not like the other high priests. He is a high priest who is able to sympathize with us in our weakness:

Since the children have flesh and blood, he too shared in their humanity so that by his death he might destroy him who holds the power of death—that is, the devil.... For this reason he had to be made like his brothers in every way....   **Hebrews 2:14, 17a (NIV)**

Jesus had to be made fully human—completely and totally human, even in pain and weakness. He shared with us in all the pains and weaknesses with which human beings struggle.

He was made like His brothers in every way. Why? In order that He might become a merciful and a faithful high priest in the service of God, that He might make atonement for the sins of the people. Because He Himself suffered, He is able to help those who also are tempted and are suffering. The writer of Hebrews would go on to say in Chapter 4, verse 15, "For we do not have a high priest who is unable to sympathize with our weakness, but we have one who has been tempted in every way just as we are—yet was without sin" (NIV 1984). Because of that sympathy from Jesus, we can do something that is quite incredible—we can approach the throne of grace for help!

Let us then approach the throne of grace with confidence, so that we may receive mercy and find grace to help us in our time of need.

Hebrews 4:16 (NIV)

I Thirst. The Vinegar Given to Jesus, illustration for The Life of Christ, c.1884-96 (w/c & gouache on paperboard). Tissot, James Jacques Joseph (1836-1902) / Brooklyn Museum of Art, New York, USA / Bridgeman Images

REFLECT:

Are you going through a time of need right now? Do you need Jesus to help you? He sympathizes with you in your sufferings. He is your great high priest who will abundantly and lovingly help you during this trial time. Boldly approach the throne of grace today!

_____

_____

_____

_____

_____

_____

_____

_____

_____

_____

DAY 23
THURSDAY
CAN YOU DRINK THIS CUP?

Then the mother of the sons of Zebedee came up to him with her sons, and kneeling before him she asked him for something. And he said to her, "What do you want?" She said to him, "Say that these two sons of mine are to sit, one at your right hand and one at your left, in your kingdom." Jesus answered, "You do not know what you are asking. Are you able to drink the cup that I am to drink?" They said to him, "We are able."   **Matthew 20:20-22**

Now, what cup do James and John have in mind? Why, the cup of victory. The cup of reward. The cup of prestige, power, and position—basically, the cup that speaks of vindication in this life. Our enemies will be vanquished. The Messiah will triumph over them. We will put Him up on top. Yes, Jesus, we can drink that cup of victory! Absolutely, we can drink that cup.

Jesus said to them, "You will drink my cup, but to sit at my right hand and at my left is not mine to grant, but it is for those for whom it has been prepared by my Father."   **Matthew 20:23**

Who, in fact, "sat" at the right and left hand of Jesus? Two thieves were crucified with Him on His right and His left. As Jesus indicated, later on in their lives, James and John would drink Jesus' cup—a cup of suffering— for the sake of the Gospel. Indeed, they would share in the cup of Jesus Christ through their death as martyrs for the faith, but that is not the way that they first envisioned it.

The apostles originally believed they would be drinking the cup of victory. But the true significance of Jesus' death is a victory won for eternity. There is no earthly vindication and no victory in this life before the Day of the Lord. This age has been judged by God.

Those who would set themselves up as conquering kings in this age will be brought low and humbled in the Kingdom of God. Faithful Christians have been continually surprised when the powers and governments of this world let them down through betrayal or corruption. Even the institutions of the Church become corrupted as people seek position, power, and prestige as methods for propagating their own worldly agendas.

No, this age and all its governances and institutions must incur the

judgment and wrath of God, along with all human sin. That is the cup which Jesus is asking God the Father, *"…if it be possible, let this cup pass from me; yet not my will, but Yours be done"*—the cup of judgment (Matthew 26:39).

Jesus would go on to teach James and John:

You know that the rulers of the Gentiles lord it over them, and their great ones exercise authority over them. It shall not be so among you. But whoever would be great among you must be your servant, and whoever would be first among you must be your slave, even as the Son of Man came not to be served but to serve, and to give his life as a ransom for many. **Matthew 20:25-28**

The people of this world look to authority, law, and power to solve the problems of the day. They fight for position. "It's push come to shove!" "It's who you know!" "Claw your way to the top!" Even those who claim the name of Christ often act no differently from

James and John; they seek places of prominence. Yet Jesus taught the Way of the Kingdom—transforming society through humility, love, and self-sacrificial service.

Jesus' way to greatness is paradoxical yet true: The first will be last, and the last will be first. Consider that the greatest leaders our world has ever known have, more often than not, been the most humble. Humble does not mean wishy-washy, but true to the character of Christ. The most powerful people to shape the world for good are the tireless and selfless servants of others.

REFLECT:

Who are the people in your life who inspire you the most? How do they demonstrate humility? Have you been seeking the world's path to greatness or the path of the Kingdom of God? How can you emulate the humility of Jesus today by serving rather than seeking to be served?

_____

_____

_____

_____

_____

_____

_____

_____

_____

DAY 24
FRIDAY
TAKE THIS CUP

On the night before His passion, Jesus entered the Garden of Gethsemane located on the Mount of Olives, overlooking the city of Jerusalem and the Temple of the Lord.

A "gethsemane" was a massive stone press used to crush the olives harvested on the hillside in order to extract olive oil. So the Garden of Gethsemane was a place of crushing—only that night it would be the Son of God who would be crushed under the weight of the press.

Here, in the garden, Jesus entered into a time of deep prayer and interaction with God the Father. Here is how the scene is described in Luke's gospel:

And he came out and went, as was his custom, to the Mount of Olives, and the disciples followed him. And when he came to the place, he said to them, "Pray that you may not enter into temptation." And he withdrew from them about a stone's throw, and knelt down and prayed, saying, "Father, if you are willing, remove this cup from me. Nevertheless, not my will, but yours be done." And there appeared to him an angel from heaven, strengthening him. And being in an agony he prayed more earnestly; and his sweat became like great drops of blood falling down to the ground. **Luke 22:39-44**

"Father, if you are willing, remove this cup from me. Nevertheless, not my will, but yours be done." What is the cup about which Jesus is praying? It is none other than the cup of divine judgment.

In the garden, he thirsted not for it; and yet from this point on, He surrendered to fulfilling the Father's will. His desires become the Father's desires. The bitter cup would become a heart's cry from the cross.

> *Yet it was the will of the LORD to crush Him;*
> *he has put him to grief;*   **Isaiah 53:10**

In distress and grief, Jesus cries: *I thirst.*

From the cross, Jesus thirsts for a cup to drink, the cup that completes the Father's will. As paradoxical as it may sound, Jesus thirsted for His own sacrificial death as both high priest and victim, for only through His death would the sins of the world be forgiven. The Lord's will for His Son was to bear the judgment for the sins of the world on His body and in His flesh.

> *...when his soul makes an offering for guilt.*   **Isaiah 53:11**

In drinking the cup of judgment, Jesus' soul makes an offering for guilt, redemption is accomplished. In drinking the cup of God's wrath, He drank it to its dregs. He drank it until it was dry. In that moment, He submitted to having God's wrath and His judgment borne in His body so that we would not have to drink the cup of God's judgment and wrath. Think about that. He drained the cup—empty—on the cross so that we would not have to drink it! Jesus submitted to death not only to finish the work of the cross, but also because He longed for the life that God had in front of Him. God the Father promised that though His soul was to suffer death in a crushing judgment for the sin of humanity, that though He must die, He would be raised from the dead—He would see the light of life.

...he shall see his offspring; he shall prolong his days;
the will of the LORD shall prosper in his hand.
Out of the anguish of his soul, he shall see and be satisfied;
by his knowledge shall the righteous one, my servant,
make many to be accounted righteous,
and he shall bear their iniquities.
Therefore I will allot him a portion with the many,
and he shall divide the spoil with the strong...

Isaiah 53:10-12

Over four hundred years before the coming of the Messiah, the prophet Isaiah revealed that, even though the Messiah would suffer death, on the other side of that "crushing" would be life, victory, and divided spoils. The writer of Hebrews again says that, *"It was for the joy that was set before him that he endured the cross"* (Hebrews 12:2). Jesus thirsted for what would follow the three days—the empty tomb, the resurrection. He longed to see it. He yearned and thirsted for the resurrected life even as He agonized in death on the cross.

It was for the joy and abundance of the life that was set before Him that He endured the scorn of the cross all the way to its bitter end. That's why the writer of Hebrews encourages us to thirst for the resurrection, so that we, too, might endure suffering and temptation, no matter the cost:

Therefore, since we are surrounded by so great a cloud of witnesses, let us also lay aside every weight, and sin which clings so closely, and let us run with endurance the race that is set before us, looking to Jesus, the founder and perfecter of our faith, who for the joy that was set before him endured the cross, despising the shame, and is seated at the right hand of the throne of God.

Consider him who endured from sinners such hostility against himself, so that you may not grow weary or fainthearted. In your struggle against sin, you have not yet resisted to the point of shedding your blood. **Hebrews 12:1-4**

REFLECT:

Whatever suffering is brought before us, whatever trials and whatever tribulations we face, we must thirst for the joy that is set before us in the resurrected and eternal life so that we can persevere in faith and faithfulness all the way to the end. How can this biblical mindset help you through whatever you are facing today?

_____

_____

_____

_____

_____

_____

_____

_____

_____

DAY 25
SATURDAY
THIRSTY FOR LIVING WATER

In the Gospel of John, we see the idea of thirsting long before Jesus utters those words, *"I thirst."*

When Jesus went to a well (called Jacob's well), He encountered a Samaritan woman there. The text tells us that Jesus sat down by the well and that He was tired, as one would imagine after a long walk. When the Samaritan woman came to draw water, Jesus said to her, *"Will you give me a drink?"*

The disciples had gone into town to buy food. That is not what Jesus wanted; He wanted something to drink. When they came back with food, He essentially said to them, "I don't need that because I have food to eat that you don't know about." They wondered, who brought Him the food?

No, what Jesus wanted was something to drink. He asked the Samaritan woman for this drink, and she was surprised by it.

The Samaritan woman said to him, "You are a Jew and I am a Samaritan woman. How can you ask me for a drink?" (For Jews do not associate with Samaritans.)

Jesus answered her, "If you knew the gift of God, and who it is that asks you for a drink, you would have asked him, and he would have given you living water."

"Sir," The woman said: "you have nothing to draw with and the

well is deep. Where can you get this living water? Are you greater than our father Jacob, who gave us the well and drank from it himself, as did also his sons and his flocks and herds?"

And Jesus answered: "Everyone who drinks this water will be thirsty again, but whoever drinks the water I give him will never thirst."

John 4:9-14 (NIV)

The question I want to ask you is whether you thirst. If so, what are you thirsty for? Do you thirst for more out of life than what this world has to offer? Do you thirst for peace and security in the midst of life's struggles?

Jesus shared our earthly thirst. Being fully human, when He was tired, He asked the Samaritan woman for a drink of water. But even as Jesus satisfied His body's thirst for water, He used the opportunity to point to a different kind of thirst and a different kind of cup to satisfy it. It is a cup that, if we will thirst for it and long for it, Jesus promises it will make us never thirst again. It is Living Water.

A little bit further on, in John 6:35, we find Jesus picking up the theme of Living Water again. He says, *"I am the bread of life. Whoever comes to me will never go hungry, and he who believes in me will never be thirsty"* (NIV). Never be thirsty!

But notice that in order to never go thirsty or hungry again, we must come to Jesus and we must believe in Him. Do you believe that Jesus Christ is the Son of God who died for your sins on the cross? Have you put your faith in Him as your Lord? Have you confessed with your mouth that Jesus Christ is Lord and do you believe in your heart that God raised Him from the dead? Jesus promises that whoever believes in Him will never thirst.

Still further into John's Gospel, Jesus picks up the theme one more time. In John 7:37-38, on the last and greatest day of the Feast of Preparation, Jesus stood and announced with a loud voice: *"If anyone is thirsty, let him come to me and drink. Whoever believes in me, as the Scripture has said, streams of living water will flow from*

Christ and the Woman from Samaria, Maratta or Maratti,
Carlo (1625–1713)
/ Pushkin Museum, Moscow, Russia /
Bridgeman Images

JESUS PROMISES
THAT WHOEVER
BELIEVES IN HIM
WILL NEVER THIRST.

within him" (NIV). John explains Jesus' words: "By this he spoke of the Spirit whom those who believed in him were to receive."

"Whoever is thirsty, let him come to me and drink."

I thirst.

Do you know what? I thirst. I thirst for what Jesus is promising. I thirst for it for our church. I thirst for it for my family. I want it personally. I long for eternal life, and I want to be so filled up with the living water of His Spirit that it overflows to those around me. The Scriptures speak about thirsting for righteousness, thirsting for His holiness, thirsting to know Him, thirsting and desiring with all of our being to be like Him, to be faithful to Him, to somehow obtain eternal life. "I thirst."

REFLECT:

Do you thirst like that? Have you ever said, "I thirst" to the Lord? Why not say it out loud now to the Lord in a prayer from distress or longing: "I thirst. I thirst for you, Jesus! Fill me with your Living Water that flows unto eternal life."

_____

_____

_____

_____

_____

_____

_____

_____

_____

WEEK FIVE
THE FIFTH WORD
ABANDONMENT

"My God, my God, why have you forsaken me?"

Now from the sixth hour there was darkness over all the land until the ninth hour. And about the ninth hour Jesus cried out with a loud voice, saying, "Eli, Eli, lema sabachthani?" that is, "My God, My God, why have you forsaken me?" And some of the bystanders, hearing it, said, "This man is calling Elijah." **Matthew 27:45-47**

Christ on the Cross (oil on canvas), Rubens, Peter Paul (1577-1640) / Koninklijk Museum voor Schone Kunsten, Antwerp, Belgium / © Lukas - Art in Flanders VZW / Photo: Hugo Maertens / Bridgeman Images

DAY 26
SUNDAY
THE PROBLEM OF EVIL

The most vexing question humans have ever asked is related to the origin of evil. It is often phrased as a question of logic:

If God is loving and good, all-powerful, and all-knowing, how is it possible that evil exists? Why would God allow it, or worse, create it in the first place, if He is good?

Many solve this seemingly logical contradiction by denying the all-powerfulness of God (His sovereignty) over His creation. Others deny God's interaction with the created world, preferring instead to embrace a God whose creation is out of His ultimate control, or exchanging God for the impersonal forces of light and darkness, good and evil. Others have just given up on belief in God period.

The problem is, there really is no good answer to the question of the origin of evil. We will forever be both intellectually and emotionally dissatisfied with answers when we contemplate human suffering, disease, natural disasters, tyrannical rulers, human holocausts, and the like.

So when Jesus asks His burning question—*My God, my God, why have you forsaken me?*—He is also asking the universal, unanswered question of human suffering: Why?

As a chaplain at the St. Francis Hospital in Evanston, Illinois, I ministered to a man sitting by the bedside of his wife, who lay in a coma. He was grieving deeply. He shared with me that well-meaning people would often come by and give what he called platitudes. They would say, "Perhaps God is teaching you something," "This experience will help you grow," "Maybe a greater good will come from this tragedy," or "God must need her more."

The man then said something I will never forget. He said, "Platitudes never make the person hearing them feel better, only the people uttering them." How true. Much of the human suffering that we experience in life makes absolutely no sense to us. We are really uncomfortable with that! So we make up reasons to bridge the emotional and intellectual gap in our hearts and minds caused by evil.

The cry of Jesus from the cross teaches us that the problem of suffering does not make sense to our human understanding! It leaves us with the huge hole of an unanswered question:

IF GOD IS LOVING AND GOOD, ALL-POWERFUL, AND ALL-KNOWING, HOW IS IT POSSIBLE THAT EVIL EXISTS?

"Why?!?" There is simply no good answer that God has chosen to reveal to us in this life. Jesus affirms our human limitation in understanding evil by asking "Why" from the cross.

REFLECT:

Do you know someone in your life who is struggling? How do you minister to them in the midst of their pain? One thing you can do is to be an intercessor with their heart's questions. Rather than giving them platitudes to make you feel more comfortable, sit with them in the quite mystery of their pain and simply listen.

_____

_____

_____

_____

_____

_____

_____

_____

_____

DAY 27, MONDAY
THE LORD'S LAMENT

Now from the sixth hour there was darkness over all the land until the ninth hour. And about the ninth hour, Jesus cried out with a loud voice, "Eli, Eli, lema sabachthani," which is, "My God, my God, why have you forsaken me?"   **Matthew 27:45-46**

In the Gospel of Matthew, we have only this one sentence of what Jesus uttered from the cross. Jesus was quoting Psalm 22, which begins with, *My God, my God, why have you forsaken me?* Did Jesus recite the entire psalm from the cross or just this first line? There is no way to know. Interestingly, the last saying from the cross, *"It is finished,"* sounds like the last line of Psalm 22: *"He has done it."* Whether Jesus uttered the whole psalm or not, the first line says enough to convey the depth of His spiritual lament: *"My God, my God, why have you forsaken me?"*

The first phrase, *My God,* reflects the intimate relationship that God the Father has with God the Son. Earlier on in the Gospel of Matthew, Jesus offered praise to His Heavenly Father:

"I thank you, Father, Lord of heaven and earth, because you have hidden these things from the wise and the intelligent and have revealed them to infants; yes, Father, for such was your gracious will. All things have been handed over to me by my Father; and no one

knows the Son except the Father, and no one knows the Father except the Son, and anyone to whom the Son chooses to reveal him.

Matthew 11:25-27 (NRSV)

Jesus and the Father are One, as John's Gospel tells us in John 10:30. No one comes to the Father except through the Son (John 14:6). No one knows the Father, Jesus says, unless He reveals the Father to them.

There's a very intimate love between the Father and the Son, and yet here on the cross, Jesus cries out to his Heavenly Father, *My God, my God, why have you forsaken me?*

The cry reveals the abandonment of the Son by the Father. We are on the precipice of the mystery of the Trinity, so we must be careful not to over-speak. How can the Father and the Son be One if, in this moment, the Son is abandoned by the Father? Can there possibly be a tear in the fabric of the relationship of the three divine Persons of the Trinity?

The words of Scripture often strain the limits of our ability to understand and comprehend. In a real and mysterious way, the Father forsook the Son. The spiritual agony of that moment is verbalized in Jesus' prayer of lament from the cross.

If Jesus prayed such honest prayers, then surely we remain faithful if we follow His example. God knows our struggles. When Jesus became man—the incarnation—He became like us in every way, even to the point of experiencing death.

Some believers struggle with the thought of uttering honest prayers to God, as if such transparency is inappropriate or a sign of a lack of faith. On the contrary, the Scriptures are filled with prayers of complaint, lament, and even anger voiced to God in prayer.

God wants your heart, not a façade. He knows when you're struggling. Through the indwelling Spirit He has placed in your heart, He hears the groans that words cannot express (Romans 8:26-27).

REFLECT:

God already knows what you are feeling and how you are hurting. Today, go to Him with your most difficult questions, sorrows, and struggles. Engage Him with your secret pain and your heart's cry. Be honest, even about your feelings of abandonment. Jesus did. He shows us the way to pray even in the midst of our darkest hours.

_____

_____

_____

_____

_____

_____

_____

_____

_____

DAY 28
TUESDAY
THE LONELY GARDEN OF THE FATHER'S WILL

When Jesus prayed in the Garden of Gethsemane, He beseeched His Heavenly Father, *"If there be any way to accomplish redemption other than the cross, make it possible."* And yet, despite His plea, Jesus submitted obediently to His Father's will and took the cup that the Father had for Him.

As Jesus wrestled with the most agonizing submission of His life, all of his disciples failed to support Him. Three times He asked them for support through intercessory prayer:

"My soul is very sorrowful, even to death; remain here, and watch with me." And going a little farther he fell on his face and prayed, saying, "My Father, if it be possible, let this cup pass from me; nevertheless, not as I will, but as You will." And he came to the disciples and found them sleeping. And he said to Peter, "So, could you not watch with me one hour? Watch and pray that you may not enter into temptation. The spirit indeed is willing, but the flesh is weak." Again, for the second time, he went away and prayed, "My Father, if this cannot pass unless I drink it, your will be done." And again he came and found them sleeping, for their eyes were heavy. So, leaving them again, he went away and prayed for the third time, saying the same words again. Then he came to the disciples and said to them, "Sleep and take your rest later on. See, the hour is at hand, and the Son of Man is betrayed into the hands of sinners."

Matthew 26:38-45

Three times His closest friends and confidantes failed Him because of their own weakness. He desperately pleaded with them to sit with Him, to watch and pray with Him, but they were overcome by their flesh and slept.

At His most desperate hour, Jesus was left to wrestle in agony with the will of His Father, all alone. These feelings of abandonment would be compounded on the cross as Jesus cried out: *My God, my God, why have you forsaken me?*

JESUS SUBMITTED OBEDIENTLY TO HIS FATHER'S WILL AND TOOK THE CUP THAT THE FATHER HAD FOR HIM.

The will of God can be a lonely personal fulfillment. There are times where we may even question whether God is with us. If Jesus asked that question, so might we. At the end of his life, the Apostle Paul was facing the certain moment of his own martyrdom for the sake of the Gospel and the Name of Jesus. Paul discovered the lonely garden of the Father's will:

At my first defense no one came to stand by me, but all deserted me. May it not be charged against them!
2 Timothy 4:16

Notice the word all. "All deserted me," said Paul. Faithfulness to God's call is often a lonely, lonely business. However, Paul lived faithfully on this side of the cross of his Lord. While his human confidantes and friends abandoned him in his time of need, Paul knew that because of Jesus' own suffering of abandonment to death on our behalf, the Lord would NEVER abandon His people in their darkest hours. That is why Paul goes on to write:

But the Lord stood by me and strengthened me, so that through me the message might be fully proclaimed and all the Gentiles might hear it. So I was rescued from the lion's mouth. The Lord will rescue me from every evil deed and bring me safely into his heavenly kingdom.   **2 Timothy 4:17-18**

Because Jesus was God-forsaken in our place (since He embodied the sin of the world), God says to you, "I will never leave you nor forsake you." Even though we may feel times of distance from the Lord or moments where the experience of His presence is lacking, He is always with us, His people. The cross guarantees this reality. No one put this truth more beautifully than the Apostle Paul:

What, then, shall we say in response to these things? If God is for us, who can be against us? He who did not spare his own Son, but gave him up for us all—how will he not also, along with him, graciously give us all things? Who will bring any charge against those whom God has chosen? It is God who justifies. Who then is the one who condemns? No one. Christ Jesus who died—more than that, who was raised to life—is at the right hand of God and is also interceding for us. Who shall separate us from the love of Christ? Shall trouble or hardship or persecution or famine or nakedness or danger or sword? As it is written:
"For your sake we face death all day long;
*   we are considered as sheep to be slaughtered."*
*   No, in all these things we are more than conquerors through him who loved us. For I am convinced that neither death, nor life, neither angels, nor demons, neither the present, nor the future, nor any powers, neither height, nor depth, nor anything else in all creation, will be able to separate us from the love of God that is in Christ Jesus our Lord.*   **Romans 8:31-39 (NIV)**

REFLECT:

The Scripture tells you that nothing can separate you from the love of God in Christ Jesus your Lord. Nothing! That means, not even YOU can separate yourself. Think about this reality. Ponder the fact that Jesus was forsaken by God on our behalf as the bearer of all sin in order that we will NEVER be abandoned. The cross proves it!

_____

_____

_____

_____

_____

_____

_____

_____

_____

DAY 29
WEDNESDAY
ELIJAH, THE RESCUER OF THE RIGHTEOUS

The four Gospels were originally written in the common language of the Roman Empire, Greek. However, Jesus would have spoken the common language used in Israel at the time, Aramaic. While we typically have Jesus' words translated for us, in the case of this cry from the cross, we have the original. He said:

And about the ninth hour Jesus cried with a loud voice, saying, "Eli, Eli, lema sabachthani?" that is, "My God, my God, why have you forsaken me?"   **Matthew 27:46**

At least one of the reasons the Gospels provide the Aramaic saying of Jesus along with a translation is to explain to us why people thought Jesus was calling to Elijah. When the people heard those first words, *"Eli, Eli,"* it sounded in Aramaic like "Elijah, Elijah."

> *When some of those standing there heard this, they said, "He's calling Elijah."*
> *Immediately one of them ran and got a sponge. He filled it with wine vinegar, put it on a staff, and offered it to Jesus to drink. The rest said, "Now leave Him alone. Let's see if Elijah comes to save Him."*
> **Matthew 27:47-49 (NIV)**

Indeed, Elijah was the one who was known as the rescuer of the righteous. Elijah was one of the last remaining righteous prophets of God in a season when all of Israel had become corrupt. Not unlike during the days of Jesus, the very administration of the Temple and the Jewish government were all conspiring against the anointed prophets of God. Elijah lamented to the Lord:

I have been very zealous for the Lord God Almighty. The Israelites have rejected your covenant, torn down your altars, and put your prophets to death with the sword. I am the only one left, and now they are trying to kill me, too.   **1 Kings 19:14 (NIV)**

The kings of Israel were sending their soldiers against the prophet of God, Elijah. However, interestingly, Elijah never died.

Elijah was one of the two people we find in Scripture—Enoch being the other one—who was literally transported into the heavenly realms by the chariot of God. In the presence and sight of his successor, Elisha, the Lord took Elijah up to heaven without death.

GOD OFTEN CHOOSES THE FOOLISH THINGS OF THE WORLD TO SHAME THE WISE.

And so, when Jesus cried out from the cross, "Eli, Eli," some of the people who were there thought that, by calling out to Elijah, Jesus was asking God to swoop down with His chariots and rescue Him off the cross. Indeed, they believed God would do it if Jesus were a true prophet like Elijah.

The people of this world often look for a dramatic sign of God's power and reality before they place their faith in Him. And, in some of the most difficult and dark moments, God does do amazing things! Yet, most often, God chooses the foolish things of the world to shame the wise. While a dramatic rescue like Elijah's would have been a sight to see, it would have completely nullified the victory Jesus won on the cross.

Paul writes of the Jewish insistence on signs from God through mighty acts of intervention:

For since in the wisdom of God the world through its wisdom did not know Him, God was pleased through the foolishness of what was preached to save those who believe. Jews demand signs and Greeks look for wisdom, but we preach Christ crucified: a stumbling block to Jews and foolishness to Gentiles, but to those whom God has called, both Jews and Greeks, Christ the power of God and the wisdom of God. For the foolishness of God is wiser than human wisdom, and the weakness of God is stronger than human strength.

1 Corinthians 1:21-25 (NIV)

Satan once accused Job of believing in the Lord only because of the Lord's blessings. However, Job and the faithful people of God have shown throughout history that they will glorify God even in the midst of the most difficult of circumstances.

Here is the true spirit of Elijah: Elijah never forsook God, even when all others rebelled and worshiped the false god, Baal; not even when the Israelites abandoned God and His prophet, Elijah. And God revealed to Elijah that there would always be a faithful group, or remnant, of Israelites: "*Yet I reserve seven thousand in Israel—all whose knees have not bowed down to Baal and whose mouths have not kissed him*" (1 Kings 19:18 NIV).

God doesn't always show up with great signs and wonders. More often, His strength is made perfect through your weakness. In the times of seeming abandonment, as Jesus experienced on the cross, God is doing His most profound soul work in your life. The very difficulties of the fallen world are all worked into His plan of restoration and redemption. Nothing will be wasted, not even your worst experiences. God is working all things for your good (Romans 8:28).

REFLECT:

Was there a time in your life when you prayed for God to show up dramatically, to perform a sign or wonder? What happened? What was your response? Even during the darkest sufferings caused by your enemies, evil and death, God is creating the character of Christ in you. How can believing this truth change your view of your situation?

_____

_____

_____

_____

_____

_____

_____

_____

_____

_____

DAY 30
THURSDAY
THE FOLLY OF THE CROSS

Muhammad, the founder of Islam, had intellectual trouble with the cross of Jesus. Yet he wanted to hold onto the fact that Jesus was sent from God—to claim that Jesus was a great prophet, even the Messiah. [1]

So what to do with the cross? In Muhammad's logic, prophets of God were not killed in such a horrific manner. So in the Quran Muhammad wrote, "They said in boast we killed Christ Jesus, the son of Mary, the messenger of Allah, but they killed Him not nor crucified Him. But so it was made to appear to them and those who differ therein are full of doubts. With no certain knowledge, but only conjecture to follow for of a surety they killed Him not. Nay, Allah raised Him up unto Himself" (Quran, an-Nisa` 4:157-8).

Islam cannot have a prophet die such a horrific death on the cross. So it is taught that Jesus took on the appearance of one who died on the cross, or that another person died who was made to look like Jesus. Jesus, according to Muhammad, was beamed up like Elijah, that is, taken directly into Heaven, ascending unto God without tasting death. The Encyclopedia of Islam says:

> *The denial [of the Crucifixion of Jesus], furthermore, is in perfect agreement with the logic of the Quran. The Biblical stories reproduced in it (e.g., Job, Moses, Joseph etc.) and the episodes relating*

to the history of the beginning of Islam demonstrate that it is "God's practice" (sunnat Allah) to make faith triumph finally over the forces of evil and adversity. "So truly with hardship comes ease," (XCIV, 5, 6). For Jesus to die on the cross would have meant the triumph of his executioners; but the Quran asserts that they undoubtedly failed: "Assuredly God will defend those who believe" (XXII, 49). "He confounds the plots of the enemies of Christ" (III, 54).

The New Testament teaches something quite different: Jesus did die on the cross. His executioners did triumph over Him from a worldly perspective. Indeed, in the crucifixion it appears that even Satan has won and evil has triumphed. Why did God NOT defend his Christ and "confound the plots of the enemies of Christ" as Muhammad would have insisted?

Here is God's Son, the Messiah, the Anointed of God, the One on whom the Holy Spirit descended like a dove from Heaven,

JESUS, ACCORDING TO MUHAMMAD, WAS TAKEN DIRECTLY INTO HEAVEN WITHOUT TASTING DEATH.

of whom God the Father said clearly, *"This is my Son, whom I love. With him I am well pleased."* (Matthew 17:17, NIV) And yet Jesus cried out on the cross, *"My God, my God, why have you forsaken me?"*

And then He died. Breathing His last, His Spirit was given up. Indeed, it does seem that God had forsaken His Anointed. Islam cannot have such a Messiah; the world does not want such a Messiah. But God demands one.

REFLECT:

Why do you think it is hard for some people, like Muhammad, to accept that Jesus truly died on the cross? In what ways do you see the cross of Christ rejected as folly by our society or those you know? What does it mean to you personally that Jesus literally died on the cross for your sins?

_____

_____

_____

_____

_____

_____

_____

_____

_____

DAY 31
FRIDAY
THE "WHY" QUESTION

"My God, my God, why have you forsaken me?"

When Jesus asks this question from the cross—the same question that our own hearts often cry—there is actually a divine answer in reply.

The answer is not verbal, nor immediate. But it is earth-shattering. That is, in this climactic moment of Satan's apparent victory over the Son of God, evil was resoundingly defeated! In the moment of Christ's death for humanity, the power of evil was once and for all thwarted and stripped of its hold on all of us through the power of law, sin, and the fear of the grave. Yet this answer would not yet be heard for three more days.

In C.S. Lewis's *The Chronicles of Narnia*, Aslan the Lion, who is an archetype of Jesus, is put to death on a stone table by the evil White Witch. Aslan willing sacrifices himself in place of a traitorous human child. The climactic moment of the story is the instant of Aslan's death:

> At that moment they heard from behind them a loud noise—a great cracking, deafening noise as if a giant had broken a giant's plate.... The Stone Table was broken into two pieces by a

great crack that ran down it from end to end; and there was no Aslan. [2]

In that moment, the Evil One seemingly wins.

But that is not the end of the story! Death cannot hold Aslan, and his resurrection to life soundly defeats evil. The risen Aslan describes the meaning of his death:

> *"It means," said Aslan, "that though the Witch knew the Deep Magic, there is a magic deeper still which she did not know. Her knowledge goes back only to the dawn of time. But if she could have looked a little further back, into the stillness and the darkness before Time dawned, she would have read there a different incantation. She would have known that when a willing victim who had committed no treachery was killed in a traitor's stead, the Table would crack and Death itself would start working backward."* [3]

Somehow, as Jesus was utterly forsaken by the Father on the cross in dying abandonment, the archenemy of God and humanity—Satan—was suffering a withering defeat by magic deeper still. With the crucifixion of the Son of God, Death itself would start working backward.

Now, every time the Good News of the Gospel is preached, we hear the answer to Jesus' "Why" question; we know with certainty the reason God the Father utterly forsook His Son, Jesus, on the cross:

And you, who were dead in your trespasses and the uncircumcision of your flesh, God made alive together with him, having forgiven us all our trespasses, by canceling the record of debt that stood against us with its legal demands. This he set aside, nailing it to the cross. He disarmed the rulers and authorities and put them to open shame, by triumphing over them in him.   **Colossians 2:13-15**

In abandoning His Son, God nailed to the cross the record of our sins and forever defeated evil's reign over humanity!

Why would God make such a costly choice?

"For God so loved the world, that he gave his only Son, that whoever believes in Him should not perish but have eternal life."   **John 3:16**

Simply because He loved us.

REFLECT:

Have you ever wondered if God has abandoned you? This side of Heaven, you may never receive the exact answer you are seeking to the "Why" of your personal suffering. But the good news is, you can know why Jesus suffered—because God so loved you. Mysteriously, that makes all the difference to our questions.

_____

_____

_____

_____

_____

_____

_____

_____

_____

DAY 32
SATURDAY
THE DARK NIGHT OF THE SOUL

As Jesus hung on the cross, the text tells us that darkness covered the land for three hours—the hours of noon until 3:00 p.m., the sixth to the ninth hour.

The significance of the darkness could be none other than that of judgment. The Day of the Lord had come. In Amos 8:9-10, we read:

"On that day," says the Lord God," I will make the sun go down at noon and darken the earth in broad daylight. I will turn your feasts into mourning and all your songs into lamentation. I will bring sackcloth on all loins and baldness on every head. I will make it like the mourning for an only son and the end of it like a bitter day." (NRSV)

The darkness had come in broad daylight. The judgment of God against that age was being leveled upon the Son of God, utterly forsaken. As Jesus bore the pain of the cross, we first hear the cry of distress in His fleshly nature as He calls out, *"I thirst."* But when He cries, *"My God, my God, why have you forsaken me?"* we hear the cry of abandonment in His spiritual nature—the anguish of His soul.

Christian mystics have long recognized the reality of both physical and spiritual distress that often occurs in our human journey toward a deeper knowledge of God.

The 16th-century Spanish Roman Catholic poet and mystic, St. John of the Cross, wrote a poem entitled "The Dark Night of the Soul." In his prologue, he describes the poem as a portrayal of "the method followed by the soul in its journey upon the spiritual road to the attainment of the perfect union of love with God, to the extent that is possible in this life." [4] The poem is divided into two books. The first book addresses the distress of the senses; the second speaks to abandonment of the spirit.

The dark night of physical distress, such as fasting and removing our comforts, has the sanctifying effect of helping the soul detach from its dependency on the world by purifying the senses from the controlling effects of pride, avarice, luxury, gluttony, anger, envy, and laziness. The physical and spiritual manifestations of these are hindrances and blocks to union with the Lord. As the Scripture teaches, *"Man does not live on bread alone, but on every word that comes from the mouth of God."* (Deuteronomy 8:3, NIV 1984) God transforms the longing of the flesh. The thirst for earthly water is transfigured into a thirst for Living Water.

The dark night of spiritual abandonment—feeling an absence of God's presence—has another sanctifying purpose in our lives. It liberates us from the troublesome states that beguile the soul, such as depression, anxiety, grief, and other forms of despondency. One way to think about it is through the parallel of a young child working through separation anxiety. Though a parent physically leaves a child's presence, that child must learn to trust and be secure in the parent's love despite the absence, knowing the parent will return.

The same is true of a maturing relationship with God. The soul of fallen man must learn to trust and obey the Lord even during times of a spiritual absence of God's presence. Times of physical distress can actually be rich times of spiritual feeling and experience. But mature faith can even be steadfast in times of spiritual distress—when there are no feelings of God's presence or experience of His love.

St. John of the Cross describes the spiritual dark night:

> *But what the sorrowful soul feels most in this condition is its clear perception, as it thinks, that God has abandoned it, and, in His abhorrence of it, has flung it into darkness; it is a grave and piteous grief for it to believe that God has forsaken it.* [5]

The experience of the sorrowful soul can drive the faithful to deeper longing and surrender in preparation for full union with the pure flame of Divine love. All dross of attachment to the "old man," both physical and spiritual, must be burned off and refined in order that the new creation might emerge.

> *It is meet [agreeable], then, that the soul be first of all brought into emptiness and poverty of spirit and purged from all help, consolation and natural apprehension with respect to all things, both above and below. In this way, being empty, it is able indeed to be poor in spirit and freed from the old man, in order to live that new and blessed life which is attained by means of this night, and which is the state of union with God.* [6]

Jesus underwent both the physical and the spiritual dark night of the soul. The prophet Isaiah promised the Messiah that through spiritual suffering, new light of true life would break forth from the darkness—that *"out of the suffering of his soul he shall see the light of life and be satisfied..."* (Isaiah 53:11a NIV).

Those who would follow Jesus and daily walk in the Way of the Cross will eventually find themselves in the spiritual dark night of the soul. The experience of the Night is painful, excruciatingly so at times, but it produces in us its desired effect—glorious resurrection life powered by the pure love of God. St. John called it "the Happy Night."

St. John described the process of spiritual formation during the dark night of the soul as a mystic ladder of Divine love. He describes ten steps on the ladder. One might consider them steps in the growth process that reorients the soul of the faithful Christian as it is formed by periods of distress and abandonment.

Ten Steps of the Mystic Ladder of Divine Love

- The first step of love causes the soul to languish, and this to its advantage.

- The second step causes the soul to seek God without ceasing.

- The third step of the ladder of love is that which causes the soul to work and gives it fervor so that it fails not.

- The fourth step of this ladder of love is that whereby there is caused in the soul an habitual suffering because of the Beloved, yet without weariness.

- The fifth step of this ladder of love makes the soul to desire and long for God impatiently.

- On the sixth step the soul runs swiftly to God and touches Him again and again; and it runs without fainting by reason of its hope.

- The seventh step of this ladder makes the soul to become vehement in its boldness.

- The eighth step of love causes the soul to seize Him and hold Him fast without letting Him go, even as the Bride says, after this manner: 'I found Him Whom my heart and soul love; I held Him and I will not let Him go.'

- The ninth step of love makes the soul to burn with sweetness.

- The tenth and last step of this secret ladder of love causes the soul to become wholly assimilated to God, by reason of the clear and immediate vision of God which it then possesses; when, having ascended in this life to the ninth step, it goes forth from the flesh. [7]

REFLECT:

Perhaps you have been through a dark night of the soul. Perhaps you are in one now. Take a moment to recall that the Lord works His greatest acts of redemption and renewal in the Valley of the Shadow of Death. Reread the ten steps of the Ladder of Divine Love. Where are you on the ladder? What step comes next?

_____

_____

_____

_____

_____

_____

_____

_____

_____

_____

WEEK SIX
THE SIXTH WORD
REUNION

"FATHER, INTO YOUR HANDS I COMMIT MY
SPIRIT!"

*It was now about the sixth hour, and there was
darkness over the whole land until the ninth hour,
while the sun's light failed. And the curtain of the
temple was torn in two.*

*Then Jesus, calling out with a loud voice, said,
"Father, into your hands I commit my spirit!" And
having said this he breathed his last.*

*Now when the centurion saw what had taken
place, he praised God, saying, "Certainly this man
was innocent!" And all the crowds that had assem-
bled for this spectacle, when they saw what had
taken place, returned home beating their breasts.
And all his acquaintances and the women who
had followed him from Galilee stood at a distance
watching these things.* **Luke 23:44-49**

DAY 33
SUNDAY
HOPE ON THE CROSS

Jesus' sixth saying from the cross is a prayer of surrender and trust. He prayed:

"Father, into your hands I commit my spirit."

His cry is found in Psalm 31:5: *"Into your hand I commit my spirit; you have redeemed me, O Lord, faithful God."*

Out of a place of deep distress of body and soul, the Psalmist prays further in lament and petition: *"Be gracious to me, O LORD, for I am in distress; my eye is wasted from grief; my soul and my body also"* (Psalm 31:9). Out of the anguish of the dark night of the soul, the psalmist's spirit cries out to be liberated, totally surrendered to the steadfast love of God:

> *Make your face shine on your servant;*
> *save me in Your steadfast love!*   **Psalm 31:16**

Out of the depths of spiritual abandonment, God brings the soul of the believer to a place of surrender and Divine reunion. The word translated in our English versions as "steadfast love" is the Hebrew word chesed (pronounced with a guttural "h" from the back of the throat: khesed, or *ḥesed*). Teachers of the Old Testament have long recognized chesed as the primary posture of God toward humans and the essential virtue to be emulated in our lives. The Jewish Rabbi Simlai expounded: "The Torah begins and ends with chesed." [1]

God is absolutely faithful and steadfast in His covenantal love toward His people. As Paul reflects on Divine love in 1 Corinthians 13:7-8:

Love bears all things, believes all things, hopes all things, endures all things. Love never ends.

Out of the deep anguish of His soul, Jesus arrives at a place of absolute confidence in the Father's steadfast love for Him. He places His total trust in the Father through a posture of complete surrender. Through the cross, Jesus understood God to be eminently true and good—worthy of trust.

This is why Paul encourages us to rejoice in our sufferings, knowing we will discover the same truth about God:

Not only that, but we rejoice in our sufferings, knowing that suffering produces endurance, and endurance produces character, and character produces hope, and hope does not put us to shame, because God's love has been poured into our hearts through the Holy Spirit who has been given to us.

OUT OF THE DEPTHS OF SPIRITUAL ABANDONMENT, GOD BRINGS THE SOUL OF THE BELIEVER TO A PLACE OF SURRENDER AND DIVINE REUNION.

*For while we were still weak, at the right time Christ died for the
ungodly. For one will scarcely die for a righteous person—though
perhaps for a good person one would dare even to die— but God
shows his love for us in that while we were still sinners, Christ died
for us.*   **Romans 5:3-8**

The ultimate act of chesed (steadfast love) is Jesus' surrender unto
death for you! Christ died for you. He absolutely surrendered His
Spirit to His Father for your sake so that you would absolutely surrender your spirit for His sake.

REFLECT:

What is the most difficult trial you are experiencing right now? Remember that through Jesus' greatest trial, the cross, He found God to be completely trustworthy. Whatever you are experiencing, your trials will be used by God to pour out His abundant love on you. Declare this truth aloud right now: "Father, I know your love for me is steadfast! Give me faith, and not doubt, as I go through this trial. In Jesus name, Amen."

_____

_____

_____

_____

_____

_____

_____

_____

_____

DAY 34
MONDAY
THE OFFERING OF SELF

"Father, into your hands I commit/commend my Spirit."

The cry of Jesus from the cross is translated in different versions of the Scriptures using either word, commit or commend. They are both instructive.

The Oxford Dictionary defines commit as "to bind (a person or an organization) to a certain course..." and commend as "to entrust someone or something to."

Whenever we have a funeral service at our church followed by the interment of the body at the graveside or in the memorial garden, we go through two liturgical acts: the Commendation and the Committal. The Commendation is where we entrust our loved one and our grieving hearts to the Lord. The Committal is where we bind our loved one's body to its final resting place in the ground or some other location.

The actions of both commendation and committal take place on the cross during Jesus' prayer. In absolute faith, Jesus commends, or entrusts, Himself to the Father's good hands. By entrusting Himself this way, He also commits, or binds, Himself in mystical reunion with the Father. In commending Himself, He commits himself.

Jesus' dead, fleshly body would be committed to a stone-cold tomb.

Now there was a man named Joseph, from the Jewish town of Arimathea. He was a member of the council, a good and righteous man, who had not consented to their decision and action; and he was looking for the kingdom of God. This man went to Pilate and asked for the body of Jesus. Then he took it down and wrapped it in a linen shroud and laid him in a tomb cut in stone, where no one had ever yet been laid.
Luke 23:50-53

But in His prayer, Jesus is not speaking about the commitment of His body to a grave, as we do in the funeral service. Jesus focuses on the continuance of His life! He commits His Spirit to reunion with the Father. The body of Jesus is mortal, but His Spirit is not.

The same is true of us. Our bodies are mortal. No matter how committed we are to proper stewardship of our bodies, to keeping them healthy, strong, and alive, they are finite, limited in use, and doomed to fail us.

WE ARE MORE THAN OUR BODIES. WE HAVE A SPIRITUAL NATURE GIVEN TO US BY GOD.

However, we are more than our bodies. We have a spiritual nature given to us by God.

The care and stewardship of our spirits is of much greater importance than the care of our physical wellbeing. Our spirits are made for eternal life! This is why Paul writes to his young protégé Timothy:

...for while bodily training is of some value, godliness is of value in every way, as it holds promise for the present life and also for the life to come.   **1 Timothy 4:8**

Soul care begins with a commitment. Have you made the first commitment of completely and totally entrusting your spirit to the good hands of the Father and His covenantal love? Total surrender is difficult.

REFLECT:

Are you ready to entrust yourself fully to God? To bind yourself to Him for eternity? This can be a scary step. Why is this? How can Jesus' example on the cross help you overcome this fear? Ask God to help you by His Spirit to commend and commit your life to Him now.

_____

_____

_____

_____

_____

_____

_____

_____

_____

DAY 35
TUESDAY
THE INNOCENCE OF JESUS

One of the main emphases in the Gospel of Luke is the innocence of Jesus. In the other gospels, this isn't as prominent a theme. But Luke picks up the theme of Jesus' innocence and highlights it over and over again.

For example, in Jesus' appearance before Pontius Pilate, Luke records Pilate's words:

- *"I find no guilt in this man."*   **Luke 23:4**

- *"...I did not find this man guilty of any of your charges against him."*   **Luke 23:14**

- *"Look, nothing deserving death has been done by him."*
                                                       Luke 23:15

Herod, the text says, agrees with Pilate that there is no basis for a charge against Jesus. What Luke is trying to convey is that Jesus is innocent, and that the rulers knew it.

In the conversation between the two thieves being crucified next to Jesus, one thief derides Jesus, saying, *"Are you not the Christ? Save yourself and us!"* Luke records the other thief as reproving him, saying, *"Do you not fear God, since you are under the same sentence of condemnation? And we indeed justly, for we are receiving the due reward of our deeds; but this man has done nothing wrong"* (Luke 23:40-41). The second thief, like Pilate and Herod, recognized Jesus' innocence.

Consider the contrast with the other gospels. Do you recall what the centurion at the foot of the cross says about Jesus at the moment of His death? In Matthew's and Mark's Gospels, the centurion says, *"Truly this man was the Son of God!"* (Matthew 27:54, Mark 15:39). Yet Luke records him as saying: *"Truly this man was innocent!"* Why? Why the emphasis on the innocence of Jesus by the Gospel writer Luke?

I believe it is related to the other prisoner mentioned in the drama—Barabbas. When Pilate said of Jesus, *"I will punish him and then release him,"* the crowd balked. They wanted Jesus crucified. Still Pilate resisted. *"Crucify him!"* they shouted. Finally, as it was the custom during the Festival of Unleavened Bread to release one prisoner, Pilate asked the crowd whom to release, Barabbas or Jesus. *"Barabbas!"* they yelled. And so Pilate released Barabbas, a man held for murder, and ordered Jesus to be crucified.

The name Barabbas literally means "the father's son." Bar is the word for "son" in both Hebrew and Aramaic. Abba means, "Father." Who else is Bar Abba, The Father's Son? Jesus! Luke is showing us that there are two "father's sons" in this story. One, Barabbas, is guilty as a murderer, an insurrectionist, and a violent man. The Other, Jesus, is innocent. And yet there is an exchange that takes place with these two men: the innocent is exchanged for the guilty; Bar Abba is sentenced to death while Barabbas goes free.

Do you see the parallel to us? We are all Barabbas. We are all "sons of the fathers." And Jesus, the Bar Abba, has changed places with us. The Father's Son, in giving up Himself to His Father's will, substitutes Himself for the other father's sons—the murderers, the violent, the angry, the prideful, the adulterous—all of us. He takes

JESUS COMPLETELY TRUSTED
THE UNJUST SCALES AND THE
UNBALANCED EQUATION OF THE
CROSS, KNOWING THAT SOMEHOW IN
THE DIVINE ECONOMY ALL WOULD BE
RIGHT, TRUE, AND GOOD.

our rightful punishment in a grand cosmic exchange of the innocent for the guilty, and we go free!

This is precisely what God, the Father, had prophesized that His Son would be called to do in Isaiah, Chapter 53:

He was oppressed and afflicted, yet did not open his mouth. He was led away by oppression, by a perversion of justice he was taken away. And who can speak of his descendants for he was cut off from the land of the living? For the transgression, which is the sin of my people, he was stricken. He was assigned a grave with the wicked and with the rich in his death.   **Isaiah 53: 7-9a, (NIV, 1984)**

Listen to this: "*Though he had done no violence nor was any deceit in His mouth*"—in other words, though He was innocent, the prophet Isaiah says, it was "*the Lord's will to crush him, to cause Him suffering*" (Isaiah 53:9b-10a, NIV, 1984). Why? Because the Lord makes Jesus' life a guilt offering, and for that reason "*He will see his offspring and prolong his days and in him the will of Yahweh will prosper in his hand*" (v.10). Think again about what Jesus has said in his sixth last word from the cross.

"*Father, into your hands I commit my spirit.*"

Certainly, entrusting Himself to God meant that He was entrusting His Father to set things right through this "perversion of justice." He was trusting God the Father for ultimate vindication, as if to say, "I can go through with this because I know Abba Father will rectify it." Jesus completely trusted the unjust scales and the unbalanced equation of the cross, knowing that somehow in the Divine economy all would be right, true, and good.

REFLECT:

Have you ever been falsely accused? How did it feel? How might your reaction have been different if you had known someone was going to make it right? Will you trust the Father today to "make right" all of the injustices and suffering you've experienced? Jesus did. Ask Him to help you.

_____

_____

_____

_____

_____

_____

_____

_____

DAY 36
WEDNESDAY
IN GOOD HANDS

"Father, into your hands I commit my spirit."

How is it that Jesus could willfully and obediently yield Himself to such a difficult and brutal plan from the Father? Only because He knew with certainty that in entrusting Himself to His Father's will, He was in good hands.

We are all familiar with the commercials for Allstate Insurance and their memorable slogan, "You're in good hands with Allstate!" The slogan has served the company well since 1950.

> *In the spring of 1950, the youngest daughter of Allstate general sales manager Davis W. Ellis was stricken with hepatitis a few days before she was to graduate from high school. Arriving home from work one night shortly after she had been hospitalized, a worried Ellis was greeted by reassuring words from his wife, who told him, "The hospital said not to worry. We're in good hands with the doctor."*
>
> *Later that year, Ellis and a marketing team were locked in an all-day brainstorming session to develop a slogan for the company's first major national advertising campaign. When the group was about to give up for the day, Ellis remembered the reassuring remarks. Then and there the slogan was born.* [2]

What does it mean to be in good hands? Do you believe that you're in good hands with your insurance company? When we say that kind of thing—and I think this is the gist of the commercial—it means something like, "This company is a good place for you to put your trust."

When we talk about a person in this way—"You're in good hands with him"— it means something to this effect: "This person is going to look after you and take care of you," or "They know what they are doing," or even "You can trust them with your life!"

We put our lives in the hands of so many people, all finite and fallen. We put our trust in so many institutions, so many organizations. And we do that with some pretty important things. We trust the good hands of the doctors and surgeons with our bodies. We trust financial planners with our life's savings. We trust teachers with the minds of our precious children. We trust pilots with our lives.

Do you see God the Father as imminently trustworthy? Would you commit your spirit into the good care of His hands? Jesus did, completely. He trusted the Father for something that will never be asked of any of us.

Do you trust God the Father completely, even when He asks you to do something difficult? When He gives you a calling that may demand your very life? We're called to offer ourselves as living sacrifices to God, holy and pleasing in His sight. Our offering is of our lives in response to this sacrifice of Jesus, in light of His mercy and His grace.

DO YOU TRUST GOD THE FATHER COMPLETELY, EVEN WHEN HE ASKS YOU TO DO SOMETHING DIFFICULT?

God has done everything to prove His love for us. So why would you trust your doctor before consulting the Great Healer? Why would you trust your financial planner before asking God what you should do with your money? And why would you trust your teachers and your government ahead of God?

Yet, many of us do. Not only do we fail to commend ourselves to the good hands of the One who is entirely trustworthy, the Lord, we also entrust our most precious jewels to sinful people who may eventually trample those jewels under their feet.

REFLECT:

What precious jewels do you need to entrust the Lord with today?

_____

_____

_____

_____

_____

_____

_____

_____

_____

_____

_____

_____

DAY 37
THURSDAY
THE SPIRIT OF MAN

In the beginning, when God created man, He formed him from the dust of the earth. The text of Genesis tells us that, *"He breathed life into him."*

Scientists have never been able to figure out the origin of life. They may have explanations (some better than others!) of how life developed once it began. But where did life itself come from?

Students of the Bible know the answer: Life comes from God. The Lord is the Author of life. He breathed life into the dust of the earth, and man was filled with the life of God. The word for "breath" is the Hebrew word *ruach*. It is onomatopoetic like its English equivalent, the word "spirit." It sounds like its meaning: ruach, breath, life. When you expire (ex-spire), you give up your spirit, your ruach.

My kids like to tell a little joke. "Is your refrigerator running?"

"Yes," you say.

"Then you'd better go catch it!"

Have you heard that one?

Here is the truth about your refrigerator: it will not run for very long if it runs too far from the outlet in the wall. That is where the appliance gets its power. The truth is—and this is no joke—your spirit has no life unless it is tied into its source of power, of life, and that is the Triune God—the Father, Son, and Holy Spirit, the Source of all life and being.

Using another metaphor, Jesus underscores this truth, comparing us to branches that need to be connected to a life-giving vine:

Abide in me, and I in you. As the branch cannot bear fruit by itself, unless it abides in the vine, neither can you, unless you abide in me. I am the vine; you are the branches. Whoever abides in me and I in him, he it is that bears much fruit, for apart from me you can do nothing.
John 15:4-5

Apart from unity with Christ, we can do nothing.

We gain our power when we commend our spirits to Jesus. For Jesus, it is union with the Father that gives Him power: *"Father, into your hands I commend my spirit."* From that moment on, everything is unleashed—power, drama, life, and resurrection! He will be raised from the dead and given new life. It is the same for us. When we offer

LIFE COMES FROM GOD. THE LORD IS THE AUTHOR OF LIFE.

our lives and our spirits to Christ Jesus, and abide in Him, new creation breaks forth:

Therefore, if anyone is in Christ, he is a new creation! The old has passed away; behold, the new has come.   **2 Corinthians 5:17**

REFLECT:

Will you commend your spirit to the Lord Jesus Christ? Unite with him. Pray, "Lord Jesus, into your hands I commit my spirit." Connection to Jesus is our source of power as we face the obstacles and challenges of this life. Plug in to Him through prayer and study today.

_____

_____

_____

_____

_____

_____

_____

_____

_____

_____

DAY 38
FRIDAY
THE FATHER'S GOOD GIFTS

I love the TV show *Extreme Makeover: Home Edition*.

Our lives are like a multi-roomed house, a disorderly house run down by the sinful, destructive forces of the world and our own unhelpful stewardship. God would have us surrender our homes to Him in order that He might give us a spiritual Extreme Makeover.

Now, we might allow Him onto the front porch or even through the front door. We might give Him a little latitude to rearrange a few pieces of furniture in some of those more public places, like the living room. But the Lord purposes an extreme renovation of the whole house, beginning with the renovation of the most secret recesses of the heart—the back rooms, the hidden closets, the places where the doors typically stay shut so no one can see the mess.

The silly thing about our closed doors is that God already knows the secrets of our hearts. Every Sunday at the beginning of worship we pray,

"Almighty God, to whom all hearts are open, all desires known, and from whom no secrets are hid: Cleanse the thoughts of our hearts by the inspiration of your Holy Spirit, that we may perfectly love you, and worthily magnify your holy Name; through Christ our Lord. Amen." **Book of Common Prayer p. 355.**

Even though we know God knows all our secrets, we still hold back huge portions of our lives from His transformational will. Why is it so hard to trust God with all areas of our lives?

It has a lot to do with the pain we've experienced from myriad betrayals of trust by other people. And it has to do with experiences of hurt and violation. We become very guarded after being hurt. Intimate relationship is risky. The issue is control. As is often said, we have "control issues." Giving in and giving control of our lives to the Lord, especially the secret places of our lives, terrifies us because it opens us up to tremendous risk.

What kind of risk? The call to Total Life Transformation. Paul succinctly sums up the call to total surrender of our lives to God and His transforming process:

I appeal to you therefore, brothers, by the mercies of God, to present your bodies as a living sacrifice, holy and acceptable to God, which is your spiritual worship. Do not be conformed to this world, but be transformed by the renewal of your mind, that by testing you

GOD ALREADY KNOWS THE SECRETS OF OUR HEARTS.

may discern what is the will of God, what is good and acceptable and perfect.   **Romans 12:1-2**

God's design is for us to commit to Him alone, like a living sacrifice—total surrender. That is what Jesus models for us on the cross:

"Father, into your hands I commit my spirit."

Our natural tendency is to conform to the worldly patterns around us, exemplified by our friends and family and the cultural environments in which we live. God desires our transformation so we can clearly see His good, acceptable, and perfect will.

Jesus promises that the Father purposes only to give you good things. He has no intention of killing, stealing, or destroying you (that is Satan's plan for you). John 10:10 says that Jesus came that you might have life and have it abundantly. The key to receiving the life of God is in surrendering our spirit to His Spirit that we might be mysteriously united in the wonderful mystery of His will.

Jesus taught us how when He said,

And I tell you, ask, and it will be given to you; seek, and you will find; knock, and it will be opened to you. For everyone who asks receives, and the one who seeks finds, and to the one who knocks it will be opened. What father among you, if his son asks for a fish, will instead of a fish give him a serpent; or if he asks for an egg, will give him a scorpion? If you then, who are evil, know how to give good gifts to your children, how much more will the heavenly Father give the Holy Spirit to those who ask him!   **Luke 11:9-13**

The Father loves you and has good gifts for you. He desires to fill you with His presence—and transform every room of your life! Entrust Him with your entire life today.

REFLECT:

Are there "rooms" in your house that you keep from God? Which ones? For what reason? Often we do that out of fear. Know today that His will is good. In order for you to receive His total transformation, you have to welcome the Holy Spirit of God into the deepest and darkest places of your life—no closed doors attempting to hide the ugly places. Let Him in!

_____

_____

_____

_____

_____

_____

_____

_____

_____

_____

DAY 39
SATURDAY
REUNION WITH GOD

My fondest memories of my childhood are of huge family reunions. Great-grandfather Holt was the father of six children. Those grown children and their progeny gathered every year for a massive tubing party down the Santa Fe River near my Uncle Manuel and Aunt Virginia's house. We had great food, fun, and fellowship. For me, it was a glimpse of the reunion of Heaven.

After his work on earth was completed, Jesus would be leaving His disciples to be reunited with the Father. He forewarned them of this coming separation:

Let not your hearts be troubled. Believe in God; believe also in me. In my Father's house are many rooms. If it were not so, would I have told you that I go to prepare a place for you? And if I go and prepare a place for you, I will come again and will take you to myself, that where I am you may be also. **John 14:1-3**

Jesus knew that the days, weeks, and years ahead would be incredibly difficult for the disciples. Not only was He leaving them, but they also would undergo the same persecution that He had suffered. The ruler of the world would marshal his forces against them. Jesus said,

Remember the word that I said to you: 'A servant is not greater than his master.' If they persecuted me, they will also persecute you. If they kept my word, they will also keep yours.　　　**John 15:20**

In this world, there will be trouble, trial, temptation, and tribulation. Jesus has overcome the world through His cross and resurrection. What awaits those who commit their lives completely to Him is a joyous reunion. In my Father's house are many rooms. Jesus is preparing a place to receive us when it is time to be home.

Do you long for reunion? Every Sunday morning, we gather corporately in worship and fellowship for a brief time of union with God and one another. Those moments of gathering are to be times of joy and mutual strengthening as we go through the time of trial.

The Adoration of the Mystic Lamb, from the Ghent Altarpiece, lower half of central panel, 1432 (oil on panel) (see 472324), Eyck, Hubert (c.13701426) & Jan van (13901441) / St. Bavo Cathedral, Ghent, Belgium / © Lukas Art in Flanders VZW /.Bridgeman Images

The Scripture promises that one day we will be reunited with the great multitude of our eternal family. It says that the reunion will be a joyous, celebration-like wedding feast—only at this wedding feast, we will be the ones getting married. We will be drawn right into the center of the celebration as Jesus is united with His church (the Bride of Christ) for eternity in the home where righteousness dwells.

After this I looked, and there before me was a great multitude that no one could count, from every nation, tribe, people and language, standing before the throne and before the Lamb. They were wearing white robes and were holding palm branches in their hands. And they cried out in a loud voice:

> *"Salvation belongs to our God,*
> *who sits on the throne,*
> *and to the Lamb."*
> *Then one of the elders asked me, "These in white robes—who are they, and where did they come from?"*
> *I answered, "Sir, you know."*
> *And he said, "These are they who have come out of the great tribulation; they have washed their robes and made them white in the blood of the Lamb. Therefore,*
> *they are before the throne of God*
> *and serve Him day and night in his temple;*
> *and He who sits on the throne*
> *will shelter them with His presence.*
> *Never again will they hunger;*
> *never again will they thirst.*
> *The sun will not beat down on them,*
> *nor any scorching heat.*
> *For the Lamb at the center of the throne*
> *will be their shepherd;*
> *he will lead them to springs of living water.*
> *And God will wipe away every tear from their eyes."*

Revelation 7:9-10, 13-17 (NIV)

REFLECT:

What positive memories do you have of a reunion? What are some of the images in your mind from that time? Read the passage from Revelation again. What images of our reunion with Jesus are the most powerful for you?

_____

_____

_____

_____

_____

_____

_____

_____

_____

_____

_____

WEEK SEVEN
THE SEVENTH WORD
TRIUMPH

"It is finished!"

After this, Jesus, knowing that all things had already been accomplished, to fulfill the Scripture, said, "I am thirsty." A jar full of sour wine was standing there; so they put a sponge full of the sour wine upon a branch of hyssop and brought it up to his mouth. Therefore when Jesus had received the sour wine, he said, "It is finished!" And he bowed his head and gave up his spirit.

John 19:28-30

DAY 40
SUNDAY
ON FINISHING WELL

I want to explore with you the traits of one who finishes well by reflecting on Jesus' words: *"It is finished!"*

Don Sweating, the president of Reformed Theological Seminary, has a pastor's heart. His dad is also a pastor, now in his 80s. Don went to him and said, "Dad, I want you to write a book."

His dad said, "Oh, I've written books."

Don said, "No, you need to write another book."

His father had written two books already. One was about how to begin the Christian life. The second book was on how to continue in the Christian life.

Don said, "Dad, you need to write a third book to finish the trilogy. Write *How to Finish the Christian Life.*"

Don's father said, "Well, I already wrote a book on the joy of getting older."

Don replied, "No, that's not it. You need to complete the trilogy with *How to Finish the Christian Life.*"

Finally Don's father said, "Well, I don't even have a computer, but I'll do it!" So, together, Don and his father wrote a great little book called *Finishing the Christian Life.*

Many of us have multiple projects going on, and they just keep growing in number—projects that we've started, that is. But do we finish them? Why is it so hard to finish well?

Frequently, I find myself captured by the tyranny of the urgent. For me, the important mission, the critical projects often get sidelined. I constantly have to reset and focus on finishing the tasks God has called me to complete in my life.

In Jesus, we see a driving intensity. In Luke's Gospel, we read an interesting verse about the resolve of our Lord: *When the days drew near for him to be taken up, he set his face to go to Jerusalem.* **Luke 9:51**

IN JESUS, WE SEE A DRIVING INTENSITY... A PERSON OF STEEL AND BACKBONE.

Jesus is a person of steel and backbone. He would go to the cross and complete the work that God had given Him to do. He had a determination to do it. If we are to be people who finish, we must be like the Energizer Bunny. We need to keep going and going and going in spite of the external obstacles, and in the face of our own internal weakness.

The Apostle James calls it "steadfastness":

Count it all joy, my brothers, when you meet trials of various kinds,
for you know that the testing of your faith produces steadfastness.
And let steadfastness have its full effect, that you may be perfect and
complete, lacking in nothing.   **James 1:2-4**

James teaches that steadfastness is the fruit of persevering through
the trials and testing of our faith. The trial and struggle to finish
builds the character that God would see in his people. It may seem
strange to find joy in the midst of trials and tribulations, but James
encourages us to see them as opportunities for personal growth in
holiness and into the fullness of the character of Christ.

REFLECT:

Are there major projects in your life that you started but never finished? Why not ask God what He would have you finish. How can you begin to build the trait of steadfastness in your life, as Jesus had? Ask Him to help you.

_____

_____

_____

_____

_____

_____

_____

_____

_____

_____

DAY 41
MONDAY
ENTANGLEMENTS

Therefore, since we are surrounded by such a great cloud of witnesses, let us throw off everything that hinders and the sin that so easily entangles. And let us run with perseverance the race marked out for us, fixing our eyes on Jesus, the pioneer and perfecter of faith. For the joy set before him he endured the cross, scorning its shame, and sat down at the right hand of the throne of God.

Hebrews 12:1-2 (NIV)

Consider Jesus as the supreme example of a finisher.

He had a pure, undivided heart that was focused on the joy set before Him. He would not be hindered by the "sin that so easily entangles" but, rather, was able to say in victory as His final word from the cross:

It is finished!

Jesus demonstrated a focused heart that would not be sabotaged by His own pain, struggle, weakness, or distraction. His deep desire was only to please the Father and win the prize.

Paul called a young leader named Timothy to have an undivided heart for God, like a soldier whose aim is only to please his commanding officer. *"No soldier gets entangled in civilian pursuits, since his aim is to please the one who enlisted him"* (2 Timothy 2:4).

In the above passage, the writer of Hebrews describes it as *"the sin that so easily entangles."* It is so easy to get caught up in the weeds of our own untended sin garden.

Yet we, as followers of Jesus Christ, are called to get rid of all the things that might entangle us or hold us back from finishing the race, especially our own sin. In persevering, we triumph over their power and hold in our lives. Jesus triumphs over the spiritual forces of evil as His people are persevering in the face of evil and sin.

How many times have you said, "I am finished, I am done, I just cannot do this anymore, I quit"? What are the snares and frustrations that brought you to that point? Sometimes it's the well-meaning agendas of other people that lead us off track or dominate our time. And sometimes, it's our own issues or sin that hinders us. What prevents you from finishing? Identify the entanglements, and singularly focus on pleasing Jesus Christ alone! The desire is to please an audience of One.

HOW MANY TIMES HAVE YOU SAID, "I AM FINISHED, I AM DONE, I JUST CANNOT DO THIS ANYMORE, I QUIT"?

A trait of a finisher is an undivided heart. Having an undivided heart to please only Jesus will free you up for a focused pursuit of His good, pleasing, and perfect will for you.

REFLECT:

How can you regain the focus that pleases God alone? What sin in your life is so easily entangling your heart? Is it your own sin? Or is it the sin of others? The Lord would hear you say with Jesus, "It is finished!"

_____

_____

_____

_____

_____

_____

_____

_____

_____

_____

DAY 42
TUESDAY
THE ADVERSARY

God is not the only one who has a plan for your life! We have an adversary, Satan (the devil), who has schemes, traps, and tricks. He tries to get us off track and prevent us from completing the work that we have been called by God to do. The Apostle Peter warns:

Be alert and of sober mind. Your enemy the devil prowls around like a roaring lion looking for someone to devour.   **1 Peter 5:8 (NIV)**

Satan's primary tool is the temptation to self-sabotage. Remember when Satan took Jesus to the pinnacle of the Temple and tempted Jesus to throw Himself off? He challenged Jesus to take a suicidal, self-destructive leap! How many times do we sabotage ourselves? The evil one does not change his tactics. He is always trying to move us into self-destructive behaviors. The problem is that we fall for it.

Some of these temptations actually come in the form of opportunities. But opportunities can be distractions from the primary task God has called you to do. The devil may also try to get you to do things in improper timing. Remember when Jesus' mother urged Him to perform the miracle at the wedding feast of Cana? He answered her, "It's not the right time."

Jesus also was very clear with His disciples about what He had to do, the work He had been called to do, when He said, I am going to suffer at the hands of the chief priest and the scribes. I'm going to Jerusalem. I'm going to die and then three days later, I'm going to rise from the dead (Matthew 16:21).

What did Peter, His best friend, say about that? *"Lord! This shall never happen to you"* (Matthew 16:22). In other words, I've got some advice, and my advice is that you should just call off the crucifixion. That doesn't sound like a good idea, Jesus.

Those who love you the most can sometimes be like Peter. They're looking out for you, but they can get you off task for fear of your well-being. Jesus threw Peter's words off instantly.

"Get behind me, Satan!" (Matthew 16:23).

Yes, Peter was a friend. But at that moment, Peter spoke the devil's sabotaging words into Jesus' life. Peter's words came in the form of human solutions, earthly kingdoms, quick fixes, and even protective concern. Sometimes Satan's sabotage comes through just such advice from those we love or even from our own hearts. Our fears and our own avoidance of pain, hard work, and struggle can pull us off the path.

Satan is sneaky and tricky. He wants to stop us from fulfilling God's call in our life, and he does it in very subtle ways, often through the temptation to other good things—but things that ultimately pull us off course. The bottom line for Satan is that he does not want you to finish! Don't ever underestimate him. Every Christian who finishes the race well is another reminder to Satan of his ultimate defeat. He will stop at nothing to try to stop you from finishing.

Hear how the thief on the cross and those nearby were used by Satan to tempt Jesus not to finish His race:

"Are you not the Christ? Save yourself and us!" Luke 23:39

Rather, they should have encouraged the One running the ultimate race on behalf of all humanity saying, "If you are the Christ, finish the work that you have been called to do! Go, Jesus, go!" In finishing the work, Jesus triumphed over Satan and the powers of evil. Satan did not want Jesus to finish, and he does not want you to finish well.

The voice of Satan is always tempting and taunting you to quit. Let the words of James encourage you:

Resist the devil, and he will flee from you. Draw near to God, and he will draw near to you.   **James 4:7-8**

REFLECT:

How is Satan tempting you right now to give up on the race set before you? What are the things that Satan uses—his strategies, the little temptations to sin in your life? What is he doing to distract you from fulfilling your call?

_____

_____

_____

_____

_____

_____

_____

_____

_____

_____

DAY 43
WEDNESDAY
A FOCUSED PURSUIT (THE "IT" FACTOR)

Finishing well requires a focused pursuit, or what you might call a vision. Consider Jesus' statement:

It is finished!

What is the "it" that Jesus needed to finish? What is the "it" factor?

Going back to John 17:4, Jesus says this: *I glorified you on earth, having accomplished the work that you gave me to do.*

The "it" for Jesus was the work the Father had given Him to do. Jesus had a calling, a vocation, a task to accomplish. That work included stress, denials by friends, bleeding, mocking, the shedding of tears, and an excruciating, painful, and crushing death on the cross. That was the work the Father had given Him to do! In finishing all those horrific things, He completed a task that would bring redemption and salvation to the world.

As tough as Jesus' vocation was, it was absolutely essential that it be accomplished. If it were not, there would be no atonement for sins, no redemption of our souls, and no salvation for us. But Halleluiah, it was accomplished! Jesus could say, *"It is finished!"*

I want to ask you a very important question. It's perhaps the most important question you could ever ask yourself after giving your heart to Jesus: What is the "it" for your life? What is the work that God has given you to do? Do you know? Because if you don't know what it is—you will not be working to accomplish and finish it.

Where there is no vision, the people perish... **Proverbs 29:18 (KJV)**

If you cannot answer that question, you may be accomplishing many good things, but leaving the most important thing incomplete. What a sad thing to die having not completed the work that God put you on this earth to accomplish!

You might call it single-mindedness. Paul describes it this way:

But one thing I do: forgetting what lies behind and straining forward to what lies ahead, I press on toward the goal for the prize of the upward call of God in Christ Jesus.

Philippians 3:13-14

Do we say, like Paul, *"But one thing I do.... I press on toward the goal of the upward call of God in Christ Jesus"?* I think many of us say, "This is one of the fifty things I dabble in to keep myself busy." But not Paul!

WHAT IS THE "IT" FOR YOUR LIFE? WHAT IS THE WORK THAT GOD HAS GIVEN YOU TO DO?

Not Jesus! The Scriptures do not teach that the key to the Christian life is busyness.

Jesus focused on the "it." *"It is finished!"* You are not finished until "it" is finished.

REFLECT:

What is the "one thing" God has given you to do in this life? If you do not know the answer to that question, ask God in prayer, "What on earth am I here for?" And then listen. The answer may be immediate or it may take a season of listening. But when you know "it," set your mind on that vision and finish it!

_____

_____

_____

_____

_____

_____

_____

_____

_____

DAY 44
THURSDAY
A DRIVING INTENSITY

An example in the Old Testament of one who was a great finisher is a man named Caleb. Caleb was one of the warriors of God who was with Joshua and the other spies when the Israelites first arrived at the threshold of the Promised Land.

First, it did not take the Israelites forty years to get to the Promised Land! That may be a surprise to read. They arrived there quickly but stopped on the threshold. They sent a group of spies over the Jordan River into the Promised Land to investigate. The spies came back with a mixed report. They admitted the place was everything God said it was, a land filled with milk and honey. (They even brought back pomegranates and some other small treasures.) But the report had another side:

So they brought to the people of Israel a bad report of the land that they had spied out, saying, "The land, through which we have gone to spy it out, is a land that devours its inhabitants, and all the people that we saw in it are of great height... and we seemed to ourselves like grasshoppers, and so we seemed to them." **Numbers 13:32-33**

Grasshoppers. That's how these spies felt in comparison to "giants" they had seen in the land. Bad news travels fast, and news of the giants spread like wildfire through the Israelite camp. Everyone started to grumble against Moses and Aaron, saying, "What did you do, bringing us to this land just to get us killed?"

But two of the spies, Caleb and Joshua, said, "NO! It's a good land. And it's our land. Let's go. God is with us!" While the others grumbled and whined about the difficulty of the task, Caleb and Joshua showed the character of single-mindedness. They wanted to be finishers. But the Israelites listened to the voice of fear instead, and God required the Israelites to do forty years of laps around the desert.

In the book of Joshua, we pick back up with the story of Caleb again. After forty years of wandering, the Israelites had started to conquer the land under the leadership of Joshua, but things grew difficult. The strongholds of the groups identified by the spies held fast. The Israelites could not vanquish them. They started to give up on these tougher assignments and tougher jobs. They started to falter. They started to quit.

By then, Caleb was 85 years old. Here is the character of driving intensity, from Joshua 14:

Then the people of Judah came to Joshua at Gilgal. And Caleb the

IT DID NOT TAKE THE ISRAELITES FORTY YEARS TO GET TO THE PROMISED LAND!

son of Jephunneh the Kenizzite said to him, "You know what the LORD said to Moses the man of God in Kadesh-barnea concerning you and me. I was forty years old when Moses the servant of the LORD sent me from Kadesh-barnea to spy out the land, and I brought him word again as it was in my heart.   **Joshua 14:6-7**

Hear the character of determination that Caleb manifests; he had convictions.

But my brothers who went up with me made the heart of the people melt; yet I wholly followed the LORD my God. And Moses swore on that day, saying, 'Surely the land on which your foot has trodden shall be an inheritance for you and your children forever, because you have wholly followed the LORD my God.'   **Joshua 14:8-9**

Caleb was basically saying this: "It's time for me to claim the Lord's promise. God kept me alive for 45 years since we first spied the land while Israel moved about in the desert. So here I am today, 85 years old, and I'm still as strong today as the day Moses first sent me up."

Caleb was as vigorous to go out to battle at age 85 as he was when he was 40. Now give me this hill country that the Lord promised me that day!!

You heard him. Caleb was a finisher. I love the way the story ends.

"Then Joshua blessed Caleb son of Jephunneh and gave him Hebron as his inheritance." (Joshua 14:13)…and there's this little parenthetical statement at the end of the story here: *"Now the name of Hebron formerly was Kiriath-arba. (Arba was the greatest man among the Anakim)"* (Joshua 14:15). Not any more. It is called Hebron now because Caleb changed the name after he went up there and defeated the mighty Arba. Caleb finished the job of conquering the toughest part of the Promised Land—the place of the "giants."

How? Caleb had determination in the strength of the Lord. "Give me those hills!" Caleb claimed lands for the Lord at 85 years old.

REFLECT:

Do you have a driving intensity like Caleb? Do you yearn to finish what God has put you on this earth to do? It doesn't matter how old or young you are. What matters is that you have a fire in your bones that says, "Give me that hill country!" That is how you will accomplish your call.

DAY 45
FRIDAY
FAITH TO OVERCOME

The final characteristic needed is a certain confidence; we call it faith.

No one said that finishing the task for which God has put us on this earth is going to be easy. In fact, the Scriptures warn that it's not going to be easy. It's going to require a certain characteristic that will get us through the most difficult challenges and obstacles in this world. The evil one and all the forces of Satan that are marshaled against God will throw obstacles at God's people to prevent us from finishing the task we've been given to do.

It will be tempting to give up, to quit. That's why we have to have a confidence that comes from outside of ourselves, something that will give us the strength to persevere and to stay single-minded when the going gets tough. Where does that kind of strength come from?

Jesus is the outside source of our strength. It takes enduring faith to finish well, but not faith in ourselves as the self-help books maintain. They encouraging you to "Believe in yourself" or "Increase your self-esteem." That doesn't work. You can't pull yourself up by your own bootstraps. You need somebody else to strengthen you.

There's a stained glass window at my church, St. Peter's in Lake Mary, Florida, that portrays the Apostle Peter trying to walk on the water. It captures the moment when Peter looks at the wind and takes his eyes off Jesus. Right then, he starts to sink:

And Peter answered him, "Lord, if it is you, command me to come to you on the water." He said, "Come." So Peter got out of the boat and walked on the water and came to Jesus. But when he saw the wind, he was afraid, and beginning to sink he cried out, "Lord, save me." Jesus immediately reached out his hand and took hold of him, saying to him, "O you of little faith, why did you doubt?"

Matthew 13:28-31

But as soon as Peter turns his eyes back to the Lord, he rises up again and walks on the water once more!

Jesus is our focus. He is our strength. And He is also an example of what we are to seek. Listen to what He said:

I can do nothing on my own. As I hear, I judge, and my judgment is just, because I seek not my own will but the will of him who sent me.

John 5:30

If Jesus says, "I can do nothing on my own," what in the world makes us think that we somehow can do life on our own?! If Jesus constantly sought His Father's will and not His own, shouldn't we do the same?

What is the Father's work that you have been given to do? It's not your work. It's not somebody else's assignment for you. It's from none other than the Lord. That's why He is the one you have to trust: the Father. Whatever He has called you to do, it's faith in the Father and faith in Jesus (the Author and Perfecter of our faith) that will get you through.

I love this little poem about a young boy in a race who keeps falling down, desperately wanting to please his dad:

> *Defeat! He lay there silently, a tear dropped from his eye.*
> *"There's no sense in running anymore...I'm out...why try?*
> *I've lost, so what's the use," he thought, "I'll live with my disgrace."*
> *But then he thought about his Dad he'd soon have to face.*
> *"Get up," an echo sounded low, "Get up and take your place."*
> *"You were not meant for failure here, so get up and finish the race"* ...
> *He resolved that win or lose, at least he would not quit...*
> *And to his Dad he sadly said, "I didn't do so well."*
> *"To me, you won," his father said. "You rose each time you fell."*
> *And now when things seem dark and hard and difficult to face,*
> *the memory of that little boy helps me in my race.*
> *For all of life is like that race, with ups and downs and all,*
> *And all you have to do to win—is rise each time you fall.*
> *"Quit! Give up, you're beaten," they still shout in my face.*
> *But another voice within me says, "Get up and win that race."* [1]

"It is finished!"

In the last book of the Bible, there are seven letters to seven churches, and in those letters, Jesus makes a final point to every one of those churches. Over and over, He says: *"To him who overcomes... to him who overcomes...to him who overcomes...and to every one of those who overcome..."*

What does Jesus promise to those who overcome?

Here is a montage of all of the promises to overcomers:

I will give the right to eat from the tree of life, which is in the Paradise of God. He who overcomes will not be hurt at all by the second death. To him who overcomes, I will give some of the hidden manna. To

him who overcomes and does my will to the end, I will give author-
ity over the nations. He who overcomes like them will be dressed
in white. I will never blot out his name from the Book of Life, but
will acknowledge his name before my Father and his angels. Hold
on to what you have so that no one will take your crown. Him who
overcomes, I will make a pillar in the temple of my God. To him who
overcomes, I will give the right to sit with me on my thrown just as I
overcame and sat down with my Father on his throne." [2]

Here are the prizes promised to those who finish: the Paradise of
God, the right to eat from the tree of life, immunity from the pain
of the second death, the gift of some hidden manna.

I am not sure what some of that means, but it all sounds awesome!

And there's more: authority over the nations, dressed in white,
never blotted from the Book of Life, acknowledged continually before the Father and the angels of Heaven, a pillar in the temple of
God, and the right to sit at the Throne of God with Jesus. Imagine
God triumphing over every evil in that day!

To him who overcomes… *"It is finished!"*

Triumph.

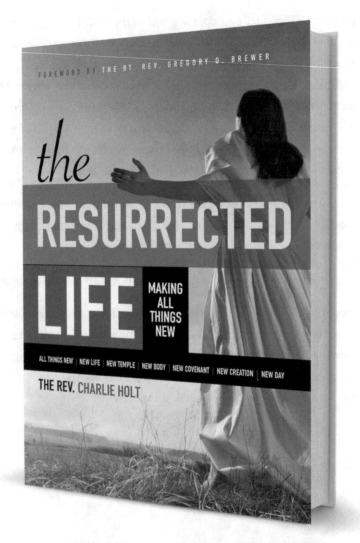

TO ORDER SMALL GROUP RESOURCES,
VISIT CHRISTIANLIFETRILOGY.COM

Bible Study Media

END NOTES

Week Two

(Page 38) [1] Kristalyn Salters-Pedneault, "What is Shame?" About Health http://bpd.about.com/od/glossary/g/shame.htm, June 19, 2014.

(Page 62) [2] "The Believing Thief," A sermon delivered by the Rev. Charles H. Spurgeon at the Metropolitan Tabernacle, Newington, England (April 7th, 1889).

Week Three

(Page 88) [1] Miriam Greenspan, "Solace: A Publication for Survivors of Suicide," Sponsored by the Alachua County Crisis Center, (Volume V, Issue 2, April 2007) p. 3.

Week Five

(Page 152) [1] See Qur'an, Surah 3:45, 46

(Page 157) [2] C.S. Lewis, The Chronicles of Narnia: The Lion, the Witch and the Wardrobe (New York: Harper Collins, 1978) p. 161.

(Page 157) [3] Ibid. p. 163.

(Page 161) [4] St. John of the Cross, The Dark Night of the Soul Book I, Prologue.

(Page 162) [5] St. John of the Cross (1542-1591), Dark Night of the Soul (Grand Rapids, MI: Christian Classics Ethereal Library) p. 69.

(Page 162) [6] Ibid. p. 82.

(Page 164) [7] Mystical Ladder of Divine Love are expanded in Book II, Chapters XIX and XX of St. John of the Cross, The Dark Night of the Soul, Third Revised Edition (translated by E. Allison Peers, Image Books, 1959)

Week Six

(Page 169) [1] Talmud Bavli (Babylonian Talmud), Sotah 14a.

(Page 182) [2] "'You're in Good Hands' Celebrates 50th Anniversary" PRNewswire, Northbrook, IL, December 20, 2000.

Week Seven

(Page 222) [1] Author unknown, Excerpt quoted in Stu Weber, Tender Warrior, (Multnomah Publishers, Inc. Sisters OR, 1999) p. 235.

(Page 223) [2] Revelation 2:7, 11, 17, 26; 3:5, 12, 21 (NIV).